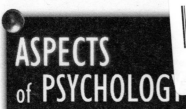

ASPECTS of PSYCHOLOGY

RHYTHMS and STATES of AWARENESS

ROB MCILVEEN & RICHARD GROSS

Hodder & Stoughton

A MEMBER OF THE HODDER HEADLINE GROUP

Dedication

To all students of Psychology: past, present and future

British Library Cataloguing in Publication Data
A catalogue record for this title is available from the British Library

ISBN 0 340 74895 8

First published 1999
Impression number   10 9 8 7 6 5 4 3 2 1
Year   2003 2002 2001 2000 1999

Typeset by GreenGate Publishing Services, Tonbridge, Kent.
Printed and bound in Great Britain for Hodder and Stoughton Educational, a division of
Hodder Headline plc, 338 Euston Road, London NW1 3BH,
by Cox & Wyman, Reading, Berks

CONTENTS

PREFACE

The *Aspects of Psychology* series aims to provide a short and concise, but detailed and highly accessible, account of selected areas of psychological theory and research.

Bodily Rhythms and States of Awareness consists of five chapters. Chapter 1 discusses several bodily rhythms, including the ultradian rhythm, the most researched example of which is sleep. Sleep is examined further in Chapter 2, including theories of its function. Chapter 3 deals with the nature and functions of dreaming, and Chapter 4 considers explanations of hypnosis and some of its practical applications. Finally, in Chapter 5 we discuss the effects of a variety of drugs which are used to alter consciousness for pleasurable purposes.

For the purposes of revision, we have included detailed summaries of the material presented in each chapter. Instead of a separate glossary, for easy reference the Index contains page numbers in **bold** which refer to definitions and main explanations of particular concepts.

ACKNOWLEDGEMENTS

We would like to thank Dave Mackin, Anna Churchman and Denise Stewart at GreenGate Publishing for their swift and efficient preparation of the text. Thanks also to Greig Aitken at Hodder for all his hard work in coordinating this project (we hope it's the first of many!), and to Tim Gregson-Williams for his usual help and support.

Picture Credits

The publishers would like to thank the following for permission to reproduce photographs and other illustrations in this book:

p10 (Fig 1.2), Dr D. Cohen; p16 (Fig 1.5), Steve Goldberg/Monkmeyer Press Photo Service; p23 (Fig 2.1), from *Psychology: Science, Behaviour and Life*, Second Edition, by Robert L. Crooks, copyright 1991 Holt, Rinehart & Winston, reproduced by permission of the publisher; p41 (Table 3.1), from *Psychology*, Fourth Edition by Spencer A. Rathus, copyright 1990 Holt, Rinehart & Winston, reproduced by permission of the publisher; p50 (Fig 3.1), The Telegraph Group Limited, London.

Every effort has been made to obtain necessary permission with reference to copyright material. The publishers apologise if inadvertently any sources remain unacknowledged and will be glad to make the necessary arrangements at the earliest opportunity.

BODILY RHYTHMS

Introduction and overview

According to Marks & Folkhard (1985):

> 'rhythmicity is a ubiquitous characteristic of living cells. In the human it is evident within the single cell, in individual behaviour, and at the population level'.

A bodily rhythm is a *cyclical variation over some period of time in physiological or psychological processes*. This chapter looks at five types of bodily rhythm and research findings relating to them.

Circadian rhythms

Circadian rhythms are consistent cyclical variations over a period of about 24 hours (the word circadian comes from the Latin 'circa' meaning 'about' and 'diem' meaning 'a day') and are a feature of human and non-human physiology and behaviour. As Aschoff & Wever (1981) have noted, 'there is hardly a tissue or function that has not been shown to have some 24-hour variation'. These include heart rate, metabolic rate, breathing rate and body temperature, all of which reach maximum values in the late afternoon/early evening and minimum values in the early hours of the morning. It might seem obvious that such a rhythm would occur since we are active during the day and inactive at night. However, the rhythms persist if we suddenly reverse our activity patterns.

The concentration of the body's hormones also varies over the day. However, the time at which a hormone is concentrated varies from one hormone to another. In women, *prolactin* (which stimulates the production of milk) peaks in the middle of the night, and this explains why women are more likely to go into labour then. Certain medications are more effective at different times of the day. Anticoagulant drugs, for example, are more effective at night when the blood is a little thinner in density, and there is a tendency for heart attacks to occur in the morning when the blood is more prone to clotting (Brown, 1996).

Ordinarily, we are surrounded by *external cues* about the time of day. These are called *Zeitgebers* (which comes from the German, meaning 'time-giver') and the process of synchronisation, *entrainment*. Folkhard *et al.* (cited in Huggett & Oldcroft, 1996) had six students spend a month isolated from any external cues. Temperature and activity levels were recorded constantly, and mood levels were measured every two hours using computer tasks. One student was asked to play her bagpipes regularly to see if the body's sense of rhythm was affected by the absence of external cues. Folkhard *et al.*'s findings confirmed the existence of several *internal* (or *body*) *clocks* or, more accurately, *oscillators* (Irwin, 1996).

One of these lies in the *suprachiasmatic nucleus* (SN), located in the hypothalamus. The SN receives information directly from the retina, and information about light and dark synchronises our biological rhythms with the 24-hour cycle of the outside world. If the SN is damaged, or the connection between it and retina severed, circadian rhythms disappear completely, and rhythmic behaviours become random over the day.

The cycle length of rhythms appears to be dependent on genetic factors. If hamsters are given brain transplants of SN from a mutant strain whose biological rhythms have a shorter cycle than those of the recipients, the recipients adopt the same activity cycles as the mutant strain (Morgan, 1995). Interestingly, the location of the transplant does not appear to be important, suggesting that the SN might rely on chemical signals rather than nerve connections.

Box 1.1 *The evolution of internal clocks*

According to Loros *et al.* (cited in Highfield, 1996a), primitive bacteria developed an internal clock from molecular machinery that responds to light so they could anticipate the coming of the sun's rays and change their metabolism accordingly. Two proteins, White Collar 1 and 2, regulate light responses, are essential to the circadian rhythm, and work in the dark without light stimulation. The proteins were first discovered in a fungus and then in the fruit fly, and it is likely that all biological clocks share common molecular components.

We can adjust our bodily rhythms if necessary. If our pattern of sleep and waking were reversed, as happens with shift-work, our circadian rhythm would eventually became synchronised to the new set of external cues. Unfortunately, some people take much longer than others to adapt to a change in their activity patterns (and in the case of travelling from one time zone to another we use the term *'jet lag'* to identify this). Indeed, we never achieve a complete reversal (Monk *et al.*, cited in Irwin, 1997). Also, not all physiological functions reverse at the same time. For example, whilst body temperature usually reverses within a week for most people, the rhythm of *adrenocortical hormone* production takes much longer.

The finding that animals transplanted with the SN of others adopt the same activity patterns as their donors, coupled with the fact that the circadian rhythm cannot be experimentally manipulated beyond certain limits, strongly suggests that bodily rhythms are primarily an internal (or *endogenous*) property that do not depend on external (or *exogenous*) cues.

One of the most interesting circadian rhythms is the sleep-waking cycle. Although some people have as little as 45 minutes of sleep each night, the average person has around seven to eight hours per 24-hour day (Meddis *et al.*, 1973). People in all cultures sleep, and even those who take a midday 'siesta' have an extended period of five to eight hours sleep each day.

The need for sleep does not seem to be *determined* by the cycle of light and darkness. For example, Luce & Segal (1966) found that people who live near the Arctic circle, where the sun does not set during the summer months, sleep about seven hours during each 24-hour period. *External* cues, then, would not seem to be of primary importance as far as sleep and waking are concerned. Of more importance is the *group two oscillator*, an internal clock which sends us to sleep and wakes us up.

Box 1.2 *The interval clock*

The interval clock is used to measure *durations*, showing how long it is since an event or process started. We use it when, for example, we determine whether there is enough time for us to cross the road before an oncoming car reaches us. The interval clock also governs time perception. The *striatum* is responsible for timing short intervals, and the *substantia nigra* acts like a metronome, sending pulses to the striatum. These two structures act like a 'gatekeeper', turning on and off awareness of time intervals, and sending this information to the frontal cortex which stores it in memory (Highfield, 1996b).

Infradian rhythms

Infradian rhythms last for *longer* than one day and have been known about for centuries. The infradian rhythm that has attracted most research interest is *menstruation*. Menstruation is an endocrine cycle, and several such cycles are experienced by everybody. However, none is as well marked as menstruation and others are much more difficult to study.

Every 28 days or so, female bodies undergo a sequence of changes with two possible outcomes: conception or menstruation. Conventionally, we portray menstruation as the *beginning* of a cycle. In fact, the menstrual period is the end of a four-week cycle of activity during which the womb has prepared for the job of housing and nourishing a fertilised egg.

The onset of the 28-day cycle is often irregular at first, but becomes well established in a matter of months. The cycle can change to fit in with events in the environment. For example, women who spend a lot of time together often find that their menstrual periods become synchronised (Sabbagh & Barnard, 1984). Why this happens is not known, but one hypothesis attributes it to the unconscious detection of some chemical scent secreted at certain times during the menstrual cycle.

The term *pre-menstrual syndrome* (PMS) has been used to describe a variety of effects occurring at several phases of the menstrual cycle. Typically, these occur around four to five days before the onset of menstruation, and include mild irritation, depression, headaches and a decline in alertness or visual acuity. One commonly reported experience is a day or so of great energy followed by lethargy that disappears with the onset of menstrual bleeding (Luce, 1971). PMS has also been associated with a change in appetite. Some women develop a craving for certain types of food, whereas others lose their appetite completely.

Box 1.3 *PMS and behaviour change*

The most pervasive social impacts of PMS are the psychological and behavioural changes which occur. Dalton (1964) reported that a large proportion of crimes were clustered in the pre-menstrual interval, along with suicides, accidents, a decline in the quality of schoolwork and intelligence test scores. However, other research has suggested that whilst a small percentage of women experience effects that are strong enough to interfere with their normal functioning, they are not, contrary to Dalton's claim, more likely to commit crimes or to end up on psychiatric wards. Any effects that do occur are a result of increased stress levels and other health fluctuations (Hardie, 1997).

For a long time, PMS was attributed to a denial of femininity or a resistance to sexual roles. However, the effects of PMS occur in all cultures, indicating a physiological cycle rather than a pattern of behaviour imposed by culture. Support for this comes from the finding that similar effects to those experienced by women occur in primates.

The pituitary gland governs the phases of the menstrual cycle by influencing changes in the *endometrium* (the walls of the uterus) and the preparation of the ovum. Timonen *et al.* (1964) showed that during the lighter months of the year conceptions increased, whilst in the darker months they decreased, suggesting that light levels might have some direct or indirect influence on the pituitary gland, which then influenced the menstrual cycle.

Reinberg (1967) studied a young woman who spent three months in a cave relying on only the dim light of a miner's lamp. Her day lengthened to 24.6 hours and her menstrual cycle shortened to 25.7 days. Even though she was in the mine for just three months, it was a year before her menstrual cycle returned to its normal frequency. Reinberg speculated that it was the level of light in the cave which had influenced the menstrual cycle. Consistent with this was his finding that among 600 girls from northern Germany, *menarche* (the onset of menstruation which occurs at puberty) was much more likely to occur in winter. Interestingly, menarche is reached earlier by blind girls than sighted girls. These findings are discussed further on page 17.

Ultradian rhythms

Ultradian rhythms are *shorter* than a day, and have been demonstrated in many physiological and behavioural processes including oral activity (such as smoking cigarettes), renal excretion and heart rate. The most well-researched ultradian rhythms are those occurring during *sleep*. Sleep is not a single state, and within a night's sleep several shorter rhythms occur.

Before the invention of the electroencephalogram (EEG), sleep could not be studied scientifically because there was no way of accessing what was going on inside the sleeper's head. Loomis *et al.* (1937) used the EEG to record the electrical activity in a sleeping person's brain. They discovered that the brain was electrically active during sleep, and that certain types of activity seemed to be related to changes in the type of sleep. It seemed that the waves tended to get 'bigger' as sleep got 'deeper'.

Box 1.4   *REM sleep*

In 1952, eight-year-old Armond Aserinsky's father Eugene connected him to an EEG machine to see if repairs carried out on it had been successful. Electrodes were also placed near Armond's eyes to try to record the rolling eye movements believed to occur during sleep. After a while, the electrooculogram (EOG), which measures eye movements, started to trace wildly oscillating waves. Aserinsky senior thought that the machine was still broken, but after several minutes the EOG fell silent. Periodically, however, the wildly oscillating waves returned. When Armond was woken by his father during one such period, the boy reported that he had been dreaming.

Aserinsky senior eventually realised that the EOG was indicating fast, jerky eye movements beneath Armond's closed eyelids, and he further observed that whilst the EOG was active, Armond's EEG indicated that his brain was highly active as well, even though the boy was sound asleep. Aserinsky & Kleitman (1953) reported that the same phenomenon occurred when EOG and EEG measurements in adults were recorded. They used the term rapid eye movement sleep (or *REM* sleep) to describe the period of intense EOG activity.

Dement & Kleitman (1957) showed that when people were woken up during REM sleep and asked if they were *dreaming*, they usually replied that they were. When woken at other times during the night, in non-rapid eye movement sleep (or *NREM* sleep), they occasionally reported dream-like experiences, but their descriptions usually lacked the vivid visual images and fantastic themes that were described during REM sleep awakenings.

The EEG allows researchers to measure the electrical activity occurring in the brain over the course of a night's sleep. Rechtschaffen & Kales (1968) devised criteria to describe changes in the brain's electrical activity. These divide NREM sleep into four stages, each of which is characterised by distinct patterns of electrical activity.

When we are awake and alert, the EEG shows the low amplitude and high frequency *beta waves* (13 cycles per second (cps) and over). Once we are in bed and relaxed, beta waves are replaced by *alpha waves* of higher amplitude but slower frequency (8–13 cps). Gradually, we begin to fall asleep. Breathing and heart rate slow down, body temperature drops and muscles relax. The onset of sleep is marked by the appearance of irregular and slower *theta waves* (4–7 cps), and we have entered *Stage 1* of sleep.

The transition from relaxation to Stage 1 is sometimes accompanied by a *hypnagogic state* in which we experience dream-like and hallucinatory images resembling vivid photographs. Such images have been linked to creativity. We may also experience the sensation of falling, and our bodies might suddenly jerk. Although the electromyogram (EMG: a measure of muscle tension) indicates that the muscles are still active, the EOG indicates slow, gentle, rolling eye movements. Because Stage 1 sleep is the lightest stage of sleep, we are easily awakened from it. If this occurs, we might feel that we have not been sleeping at all.

After about a minute, the EEG shows another change which marks the onset of *Stage 2* sleep. Although the waves are of medium amplitude with a frequency of around 4–7cps, Stage 2 sleep is characterised by brief bursts of activity with a frequency of 12–14 cps. These are called *sleep spindles* and why they appear is not precisely understood.

Box 1.5   *K-complexes*

Another characteristic of Stage 2 sleep is the presence of *K-complexes* (see Figure 1.1). These are the brain's response to external stimuli, such as a sound in the room in which we are sleeping, or internal stimuli, such as a muscle tightening in the leg. Whilst it is possible to be woken fairly easily from Stage 2 sleep, the EOG registers minimal eye movements and the EMG shows little activity in the muscles.

After around 20 minutes in Stage 2, electrical activity increases in amplitude and becomes even slower, dropping to around 1–3 cps. When these slow *delta waves* account for 20–50 per cent of the EEG, we have entered *Stage 3* sleep. After a brief period of time, delta waves will account for more than 50 per cent of the EEG and will slow to around ½–2 cps, which marks the onset of *Stage 4* sleep. In both Stages 3 and 4, we are extremely unresponsive to the environment and it is very difficult for us to be woken up. The EOG shows virtually no eye movements and our muscles are completely relaxed. Noises and lights do not disturb us as they would have done in the earlier stages of sleep.

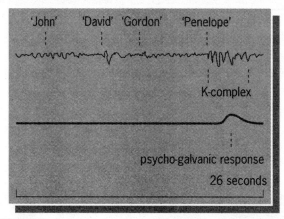

Figure 1.1 *EEG response of a person is Stage 2 sleep to the presentation of several names, one of which is his wife's*

In Stage 4, heart rate, blood pressure and body temperature are at their lowest. We have descended what researchers term the *sleep staircase* and have moved from a very light to a very deep sleep. Our first episode of Stage 4 sleep lasts for around 40 minutes. After this, we begin to 'climb' the sleep staircase, passing briefly through Stage 3, before entering Stage 2 in which we spend around ten minutes.

Instead of re-entering Stage 1, however, something very different registers on the EEG machine, and we start showing the irregular eye movements and brain activity first observed by Aserinsky. We are now experiencing our first episode of REM sleep. REM sleep occurs in all mammals except the dolphin and spiny anteater, but does not occur in fish, reptiles and amphibians, and occurs only briefly in a few birds of prey. It is therefore likely that REM sleep is related to the development of brain structures found in mammals.

Interestingly, the EMG in REM sleep indicates that the body's muscles are in a state of *virtual paralysis*, which occurs as a result of inhibitory processes (the occasional twitches of our hands and feet are presumably a result of these processes weakening briefly). The probable function of this paralysis is discussed in Chapter 3. Although our muscles may be paralysed, heart rate and blood pressure begin to fluctuate rapidly, and respiration alters between shallow breaths and sudden gasps. Males may experience an erection and females corresponding changes in their sexual organs.

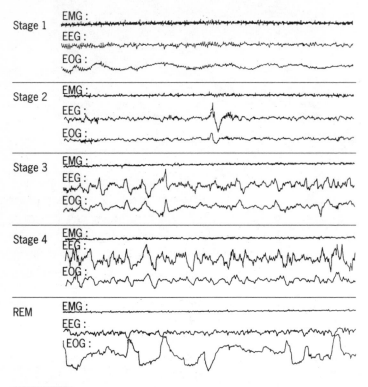

Figure 1.2   *EMG, EEG and EOG recordings associated with the various stages of sleep*

The fact that the eyes and brain of a person in REM sleep are very *active* whilst the muscles are virtually *paralysed*, coupled with the observation that a person in REM sleep is very difficult to wake up, has led to it also being called *paradoxical sleep*. Our first period of REM sleep lasts for about 10 minutes. The end of it marks the completion of the first sleep *cycle*.

When REM sleep ends, we enter Stage 2 sleep again and spend around 25 minutes in that stage. After passing briefly through Stage 3, we enter Stage 4 and spend about 30 minutes in a very deep sleep. After ascending the sleep staircase once more, another episode of REM sleep occurs which also lasts for around ten minutes. We have now completed the second sleep cycle.

The entry into Stage 2 sleep marks the beginning of the third cycle. However, instead of descending the sleep staircase (after about an hour in Stage 2), we enter REM sleep and might spend as long as 40 minutes in that stage. Again, the end of REM sleep marks the end of another cycle. Unlike the first two cycles, then, the third cycle does not involve any Stage 3 or 4 sleep. This is also true of the fourth cycle. The cycle begins with around 70 minutes of Stage 2 sleep, which is immediately followed by a fourth episode of REM sleep, and might last as long as an hour. By the end of the fourth cycle we will have been asleep for around seven hours. The fifth cycle will probably end with us waking up and for that reason it is known as the *emergent* cycle of sleep. We may awake directly from REM sleep or from Stage 2 and might experience *hypnopompic images* (vivid visual images that occur as we are waking up: cf. the hypnagogic images mentioned earlier). As was true in the third and fourth cycles, the emergent cycle does not consist of any Stage 3 or 4 sleep.

Typically, then, we have five or so cycles of sleep, each of which lasts, on average, around 90 minutes. The exact pattern of sleep varies from person to person, and what has been described is very much an 'average' since the time between REM and NREM sleep varies both between and within people. So, as well as people differing in terms of their sleep cycles, the pattern can vary within the same person from night to night. What does seem to be true for everyone, though, is that Stages 3 and 4 occur only in the first two cycles of sleep and that whilst REM sleep occurs in every cycle, episodes increase in length over the course of the night.

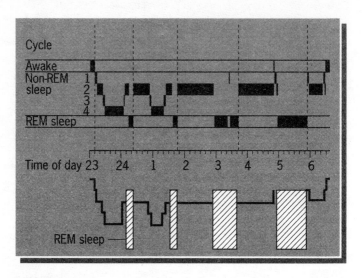

Figure 1.3 *A characteristic profile of a night's sleep. (From Borbely, 1986)*

Our pattern of sleeping also changes with age. Newborn infants sleep for around 16 hours a day and spend approximately half this time in REM sleep. One-year-olds sleep for around 12 hours a day and REM sleep occupies about one-third of this time. In adulthood, we spend only around a quarter of an eight-hour period of sleep in REM sleep, and in very old age the amount of REM sleep time decreases even further. Stage 4 sleep also changes as we get older. At age 60, Stage 4 sleep has all but disappeared. As a result, we tend to be more easily awakened when we are older even though we may have been very sound sleepers when younger.

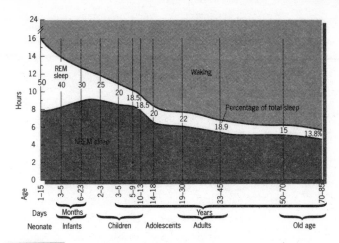

Figure 1.4 *Changes in sleep pattern with age*

Diurnal rhythms

Diurnal rhythms are rhythms which occur during the *waking day*. Whether the time of day at which a task is carried out makes a difference to how well it is performed has been the subject of much research. Because of its potential practical applications, researchers have paid particular attention to how performance of complex 'real-world' tasks varies over the waking day.

Box 1.6 *Memory and time of day*

Some evidence suggests that immediate memory for realistic events is better in the morning than the afternoon. Gunter *et al.* (cited in Marks & Folkhard, 1985) tested participants for their immediate recall of television news information. There was a decline across the three times of the day that were tested (09.00, 13.00 and 17.00). However, other research has failed to demonstrate such 'time-of-day' effects. Adam (1983), for example, found that the information remembered from lectures did not differ over the day.

It did not seem to matter whether a lecture was attended first thing in the morning or last thing in the afternoon, there was no difference in how much was remembered (or not remembered). Whilst the time of day did not affect how much was remembered,

---

Adam found that it influenced students' abilities to extract the main theme from a lecture. Students were considerably better at this in the afternoon than in the morning. Other research has shown that people tend to be better at short-term memory tasks, such as remembering a telephone number between looking it up and dialling it, in the early morning. Long-term memory seems to function better in the evening (Irwin, 1997).

Using their 'Morningness–Eveningness' questionnaire, Horne & Osterberg (1976) have argued that there are two *diurnal types*. Extreme 'morning types' are characteristically tired in the evening, go to bed early, and wake in the morning feeling alert. By contrast, extreme 'evening types' perform best in the evening, go to bed late, and feel tired in the morning. Marks & Folkhard (1985) have proposed that these differences may be due to a *phase advance* in the circadian system. It seems that morning types 'peak' two or more hours earlier than evening types on a number of variables including body temperature.

Introversion and extroversion may also be associated with diurnal differences. Such differences might be attributable to variations in sleeping and waking behaviour. Whilst the time at which we go to bed is influenced by internal factors, it can also be affected by psychosocial factors. Differences between introverts and extroverts in terms of how long they sleep and how regular their sleep is could be explained in terms of psychosocial influences (such as going to a lot of parties), and this might account for the differences between them with respect to their diurnal rhythms (Blake, 1971).

It is generally believed that differences on cognitive tasks performed during the waking day cannot be *solely* explained in terms of a circadian variation in arousal. Rather, the differences appear to be the result of a combination of many different rhythms which reflect the various cognitive functions contributing to observed performance. Exactly how the different components of the human information processing system change over the course of the day has, however, yet to be determined.

Circannual rhythms

The word circannual describes rhythms that have a period of about a year, and biological circannual clocks regulate migration, the formation of colonies, pair bonding and other seasonal changes in many species. Such changes are found in the behaviour and physiology of most, if not all, animals from temperate latitudes and are adaptive because they promote a species' survival in an environment where the climate fluctuates predictably in a rhythmic sequence (Morgan, 1995).

Box 1.7   *The circannual rhythm of the gold-mantled ground squirrel*

The most extensively investigated circannual rhythm in mammals is that of the gold-mantled ground squirrel of the Rocky Mountains. The rhythm was first noted by Pengelley & Fisher (1957) while they were studying the hibernation of squirrels. In August, a squirrel was placed in a small, windowless room which was illuminated for a period of 12 hours and then darkened for the same length of time. The temperature of the room was kept constant at 0°C (32°F).

Initially, the squirrel remained active. It ate and drank normally and its temperature remained constant at 37.8°C (98.68°F). In October, the squirrel ceased its activities and hibernated, its body temperature dropping to 1°C (33.8°F). In April, the squirrel became active again and its body temperature rose to 37°C. Finally, in September, it resumed hibernation. The alternating period of activity and hibernation typically lasts for about 300 days. The key to this rhythm seems to be temperature rather than light. This makes sense given that the squirrel, which spends a great deal of time in its burrow, is probably not much affected by changes in the length of the day.

Another rhythm which could be considered circannual is *seasonal affective disorder* (or SAD). Evidence suggests that some mood disorders are under *seasonal* control and regulated by the *pineal gland* (a tiny structure at the base of the brainstem). The pineal gland is believed to have evolved by convergence and fusion of a second pair of photo-receptors (Morgan, 1995). It secretes the hormone *melatonin*, which influences the production of the neurotransmitter *serotonin*. Melatonin production is controlled by the presence or absence of direct light stimulation to the eyes. It is produced when it is dark, but its production is suppressed when it is light. In winter SAD, melatonin production may be de-synchronised. One way of treating winter SAD is to re-phase the rhythm of melatonin production, and this is the principle underlying *phototherapy*.

Box 1.8 *Phototherapy*

In phototherapy, sufferers of winter SAD are seated in front of extremely bright lights (the equivalent to the illumination of 2500 candles on a surface one metre away being the most effective: Wehr & Rosenthal,1989). Exposure to this light for just over one hour each evening reverses the symptoms within three to four days. Since a pulse of bright light reduces the level of melatonin in the bloodstream and changes the time when it is produced, phototherapy may work by rephasing melatonin's production.

Figure 1.5 *Exposure to bright light has been shown to be effective for some individuals in the treatment of seasonal affective disorder (SAD)*

The role played by melatonin may also explain some of the findings described earlier concerning infradian rhythms. Recall Reinberg's (1967) hypothesis that the level of light influenced the menstrual cycle of the young woman who spent three months in a cave, and the evidence indicating that menarche is much more likely to occur in winter and occurs earlier in blind than sighted girls. It is reasonable to suggest that the pineal gland is somehow affected by the secretion of melatonin and that this affects both the menstrual cycle and, given the finding concerning increased conceptions during the lighter months of the year, the reproductive system in general.

Conclusions

This chapter has looked at various bodily rhythms. Several physiological and psychological effects associated with these have been identified, and some of the ways in which disruption of these rhythms can affect behaviour have been discussed.

Summary

- **Circadian rhythms** are consistent cyclical variations over a period of about 24 hours. Examples include heart rate, metabolic rate, breathing rate and body temperature. These rhythms persist even if activity patterns are reversed or external cues about the time of day removed.

- One internal clock (or oscillator) lies in the **suprachiasmatic nucleus** (SN). This receives information directly from the retina and synchronises biological rhythms with the 24 hour cycle of the outside world. If the SN is damaged, circadian rhythms disappear.

- The cycle length of rhythms apparently depends on genetic factors, and internal clocks evolved so that organisms could anticipate the coming of the sun's rays and change their metabolism accordingly. It is likely that all biological clocks share common molecular components.

- The sleep-waking cycle is largely independent of culture and the cycle of light and dark. It is determined by internal events governed by the **group two oscillator**.

- The **interval clock** measures durations and governs the perception of time. The **striatum** and **substantia nigra** act like a 'gatekeeper', turning awareness of time on and off. This information is stored in memory by the frontal cortex.

- **Infradian rhythms** last longer than one day. The most extensively researched of these is menstruation. **Pre-menstrual syndrome** (PMS) refers to the variety of physical and psychological effects occurring at several phases of the menstrual cycle.

- PMS does not predispose women to criminal behaviour or mental disorders. Any behaviour changes found are better explained in terms of increased stress levels and other health fluctuations. PMS is evidently a universal physiological cycle, independent of culture.

- The phases of the menstrual cycle are controlled by the **pituitary gland**. This gland may be influenced by (seasonal) light levels since menarche has been found to be most likely to occur in winter and is reached earlier by blind than sighted girls.

- **Ultradian rhythms** are shorter than one day. The most well-researched are those that occur during sleep. Sleep consists of a number of cycles lasting around 90 minutes. NREM sleep consists of four stages, each characterised by a distinct pattern of electrical activity.

- Stages 1 and 2 sleep are the stages of 'light' sleep. Theta waves mark the onset of Stage 1 sleep. Stage 2 sleep is characterised by **sleep spindles** and **K-complexes**. Stages 3 and 4 are the stages of 'deep sleep' and are characterised by delta waves. Stages 3 and 4 only occur in the first two cycles of sleep.

- REM sleep seems to be related to the development of brain structures found only in mammals. In REM sleep, the musculature is virtually paralysed. The brain is highly active during REM sleep, and a person woken from it typically reports experiencing a dream. REM sleep episodes increase in length over the night. In the first cycle, it lasts about ten minutes. In the emergent cycle, it lasts about 30 minutes.

- There are important developmental changes in sleep patterns. Newborns spend about half of their 16 hours of sleep per day in REM sleep. In adulthood, about a quarter of total sleep time is spent in REM sleep. This decreases further in late adulthood which is also accompanied by the virtual disappearance of Stage 4 sleep.

- **Diurnal rhythms** occur during the waking day. Research indicates that memory varies over the course of the day. Short-term memory tends to be better in the morning, whilst long-term memory is better in the evening.

- Two diurnal types have been proposed. 'Morning types' perform best in the morning and 'evening types' in the evening. These differences may be due to a phase advance in the circadian rhythm. Personality type may also be associated with diurnal differences, though psychosocial influences could be responsible.

- **Circannual rhythms** have a period of about a year. Biological clocks regulate several behaviours including migration, the formation of colonies and pair bonding. These behaviours are adaptive because they promote survival in an environment where the climate fluctuates predictably in a rhythmic sequence.

- **Seasonal affective disorder** (SAD) can be considered a circannual rhythm. Some mood disorders appear to be under seasonal control and regulated by the **pineal gland**. This gland secretes melatonin whose production is controlled by the presence or absence of direct light stimulation to the eyes. Desynchronisation of melatonin production may occur in winter SAD. **Phototherapy** is an effective treatment for winter SAD, and may work by re-phasing melatonin's production.

2 Introduction and overview

As was seen in Chapter 1, everyone sleeps at least once a day. Spending approximately seven to eight hours in this altered state of consciousness means that around one third of our lifetime is spent fast asleep! Indeed, we may need to spend as long as ten hours asleep in order to function optimally (Coren, 1996).

This chapter looks at theories of the functions of sleep. One way to study such functions is to deprive people of sleep and observe the consequences. This chapter begins by looking at the effects of total sleep deprivation and theories which have been proposed to explain the functions of sleep in general. Then, it looks at the effects of depriving people of REM sleep, and at theories of this stage's functions. The chapter concludes by looking briefly at some of the physiological processes that occur during sleep.

Studies of total sleep deprivation

It has long been known that depriving people of sleep can have detrimental effects. Indeed, sleep deprivation has served dubious military purposes over the ages. The ancient Romans used *tormentum vigilae* (or the *waking torture*) to extract information from captured enemies, and in the 1950s the Koreans used sleep deprivation as a way of 'brainwashing' captured American airforce pilots (Borbely, 1986).

The first experimental study of sleep deprivation was conducted by Patrick & Gilbert (1898). They deprived three 'healthy young men' of sleep for 90 hours. The men reported a gradually increased desire to sleep, and from the second night onwards two of them experienced illusions and other perceptual disorders. When they were allowed to sleep normally, all three slept for longer than they usually did, and the psychological disturbances they reported disappeared.

Box 2.1 *The record breakers*

In 1959 Peter Tripp, a New York disc-jockey, staged a charity 'wakeathon' in which he did not sleep for eight days. Towards the end of his wakeathon, Tripp showed some disturbing symptoms, including hallucinations and delusions. The delusions were so intense that it was impossible to give him any tests to assess his psychological functioning. In 1965, Randy Gardner, a 17-year-old student, stayed awake for 264 hours and 12 minutes, aiming to get himself into the *Guinness Book of Records*. For the last 90 hours of his record attempt he was studied by sleep researcher William Dement. Although Gardner had difficulty in performing some tasks, his lack of sleep did not produce anything like the disturbances experienced by Tripp.

Afterwards, Gardner spent 14 hours and 40 minutes asleep and when he awoke he appeared to have recovered completely. On subsequent nights, Gardner returned to his usual pattern of sleeping for eight hours per day and did not seem to suffer any permanent physiological or psychological effects from his long period without sleep.

Going without sleep for over 200 hours has subsequently been achieved by a number of people, none of whom appears to have experienced any long-term detrimental effects. This has led Webb (1975) to conclude that the major consequence of going without sleep is to make us want to go to sleep!

As interesting as the cases of Tripp, Gardner, and others are, they tell us little about the effects of *total sleep deprivation* because they did not take place under carefully controlled conditions. However, many controlled studies have been conducted. The effects of sleep deprivation over time have been summarised by Hüber-Weidman (1976).

Box 2.2 *The effects of sleep deprivation over time (after Hüber-Weidman, 1976)*

Night 1: Most people are capable of going without sleep for a night. The experience may be uncomfortable, but it is tolerable.
Night 2: The urge to sleep becomes much greater. The period between 3–5 a.m., when body temperature is at its lowest in most of us, is crucial. It is during this period that sleep is most likely to occur.

Night 3: Tasks requiring sustained attention and complex forms of information processing are seriously impaired. This is particularly true if the task is repetitive and boring. If the task is interesting, or the experimenter offers encouragement, performance is less impaired. Again, the early hours of the morning are most crucial.

Night 4: From this night onwards, periods of *micro-sleep* occur. We stop what we are doing and stare into space for up to three seconds. The end of micro-sleep is accompanied by a return to full awareness. Confusion, irritability, misperception and the '*hat phenomenon*' occur. In this, a tightening around the head is felt as though a hat that was too small was being worn.

Night 5: As well as the effects described above, delusions may be experienced. However, intellectual and problem-solving abilities are largely unimpaired.

Night 6: Symptoms of *depersonalisation* occur and a clear sense of identity is lost. This is called *sleep deprivation psychosis*.

The effects described above are psychological rather than physiological, and little physical harm follows sleep deprivation. Reflexes are unimpaired and heart rate, respiration, blood pressure and body temperature show little change from normal. Hand tremors, droopy eyelids, problems in focusing the eyes, and heightened sensitivity to pain seem to be the major bodily consequences.

Additionally, the effects of sleep deprivation do not accumulate over time. If we normally sleep for eight hours a day and are deprived of sleep for three days, we do not sleep for 24 hours afterwards. Thus, we do not need to make up for *all* the sleep that has been missed, though we do make up for some.

The experiences of Peter Tripp (see Box 2.1) are unusual. Whilst some temporary psychological disturbances occur following sleep deprivation, sleep deprivation has no significant long-term consequences on normal psychological functioning. Tripp's experiences are, therefore, unlikely to be *solely* attributable to a lack of sleep. It is more likely that *stress*, which sleep deprivation can also cause, produces abnormal behaviour in susceptible individuals.

Whilst it might be tempting to conclude that sleep has little value and a lack of it few harmful effects, such a conclusion is not justified. For example, Rechtschaffen *et al.* (1983) placed a rat on a disc protruding from a small bucket of water with an EEG monitoring its brain activity. Every time brain activity indicated sleep, the disc rotated. This forced the rat to walk if it wanted to avoid falling in the water.

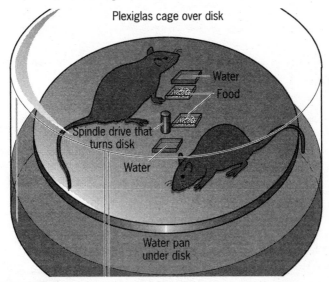

Plexiglas cage over disk

Water

Food

Spindle drive that turns disk

Water

Water pan under disk

Figure 2.1 *Apparatus used in the experiment conducted by Rechtschaffen* et al.

A second rat, also connected to an EEG, was on the disc. However, whenever its brain activity indicated sleep the disc did *not* rotate. Thus, one rat was allowed to sleep normally whereas the other was not. After 33 days, all sleep-deprived rats had died, whereas those that slept normally appeared not to have suffered. The cause of death could not be precisely determined, but given a progressive physical deterioration in the rats, the ability to regulate their own heat may have been fatally impaired.

Unfortunately, the results of sleep deprivation studies on rats tells us little about the effects of sleep deprivation on humans, and there are clearly serious ethical objections to subjecting humans to the length of time the rats were deprived of sleep. However, Lugaressi *et al.* (1986) have reported the case of a man who abruptly began to lose sleep at age 52. He became increasingly exhausted and eventually developed a lung infection from which death resulted. A post-mortem revealed that neurons in areas of the brain linked to sleep and hormonal circadian rhythms were almost completely destroyed.

Irrespective of the effects of sleep deprivation, unless we are constantly encouraged to remain awake, we fall asleep, and we do so in virtually any position anywhere. People do not like to be kept awake and there seems to be a need to sleep even though sleeplessness itself does not, at least as far as we know, appear to be particularly harmful. Again, as Webb (1975) has suggested, perhaps people sleep in order to avoid feeling sleepy. However, such a suggestion isn't particularly informative, and researchers have tried to understand sleep's exact functions.

Evolutionary theories of sleep function

Meddis (1975) has pointed to evidence indicating that different species characteristically sleep for different periods of time, and that the amount of time spent asleep is related to an animal's need and method of obtaining food and its exposure to predators. Animals that cannot find a safe place to sleep, have high metabolic rates that require a lot of food gathering, or are at risk from predators, sleep very little.

Box 2.3   *The sleeping habits of some non-humans*

The short-tailed shrew has a safe burrow, but sleeps very little since its high metabolic rate means that it must eat around the clock or die. Animals that are preyed upon, such as cattle, sheep and deer, sleep only about two hours a day, and even then take only 'brief naps'. By contrast, predator species, or those that have safe sleeping places or can satisfy their needs for food and water fairly quickly, sleep for much longer. Like the short-tailed shrew, the ground squirrel has a safe burrow but, being a larger animal, it has a lower metabolic rate and does not need to eat so often. It sleeps for 14 hours a day. The gorilla, which does not need to sleep in a burrow to protect itself, also sleeps for 14 hours a day.

In a variation of Meddis's theory, Webb (1982) has suggested that sleep enables us to conserve energy when there is no need to expend it or when expending energy would probably do more harm than good. Webb argues that sleep is an instinctual behavioural response which does not satisfy a physiological need in the way that food does. Rather, natural selection would favour an organism that kept itself out of danger when danger was most likely to occur. Sleep can therefore be seen as a response which is useful for a species' survival.

Since we usually do not walk or roam about when we are asleep and (usually) sleep at night, sleep can be seen as an adaptive instinctual behaviour that keeps us quiet and out of harm's way. This is the *hibernation theory of sleep function*. In our evolutionary past, the enforced inactivity of sleeping allowed us to survive for a least two reasons. First, sleeping at night would reduce the risk of predation or accidents. Second, since the likelihood of finding food at night would be much reduced, more energy would have been spent hunting than would have been gained by the results of hunting.

However, even though we may be quiet and out of harm's way whilst asleep, we are *potentially* vulnerable. As Evans (1984) has remarked:

'the behaviour patterns involved in sleep are glaringly, almost insanely, at odds with common sense'.

Some evolutionary theorists argue that preyed upon species sleep for short periods because of the constant threat of predation. Others argue that preyed upon species sleep for longer periods in order to keep out of the way of predators. The sleep pattern of any species can be explained in one of these two ways by evolutionary theories, which makes them *non-falsifiable* in this respect.

Restoration theories of sleep function

Safety and energy conservation could be two functions of sleep. However, whilst the neural mechanisms for sleep might have evolved to satisfy such needs, they may well have taken on additional functions. Most of us spend around 16 hours a day using up energy. According to Oswald (1966), the purpose of sleep is to restore depleted reserves of energy, eliminate waste products from the muscles, repair cells and recover physical abilities that have been lost during the day.

Box 2.4   *Sleep and energy expenditure*

The length of time we remain awake is related to how sleepy we feel, and at the end of a busy day we are all 'ready for bed'. Shapiro *et al.* (1981) found that people who had competed in an 'ultra-marathon', a running race of 57 miles, slept an hour and a half longer than they normally did for two nights following the race. The researchers also found that Stage 4 sleep occupied a much greater proportion of total sleep time (about 45 per cent) than normal (about 25 per cent), whilst the proportion of time spent in REM sleep decreased.

The restorative processes that occur during sleep are not precisely known. Some studies have shown that a lack of exercise does *not* substantially reduce sleep, which it might be expected to do if sleep served an exclusively restorative function. Ryback & Lewis (1971) found that healthy individuals who spent six weeks resting in bed showed no changes in their sleep patterns. Adam & Oswald (1977, 1983) have suggested that certain kinds of tissue restoration, such as cell repair, occur during sleep, whilst Webb & Campbell (1983) believe that neurotransmitter levels are restored during sleep.

The pituitary gland releases a hormone during stage 4 sleep which is important for tissue growth, protein and RNA synthesis, and the formation of red blood cells. This suggests that Stage 4 sleep plays a role in the growth process. As noted in Chapter 1, the total time spent in Stage 4 sleep decreases with increasing age, and this might be related to a relative lack of need for growth hormone. Disruption of Stage 4 sleep in healthy people produces symptoms similar to those experienced by fibrositis sufferers, who are known to experience a chronic lack of Stage 4 sleep (Empson, 1989). Since fibrositis is a disorder which causes acute inflammation of the back muscles and their sheaths, experienced as pain and stiffness, it is tempting to accept the suggestion that sleep serves a restorative function.

Box 2.5   *Sleep and psychological restoration*

A different approach to restoration theory suggests that sleep may serve a psychological as well as (or instead of) a physiological restorative function. For example, Kales *et al.* (1974) have shown that insomniacs suffer from far more psychological problems than healthy people, whilst Hartmann (1973) has reported that we generally need to sleep more during periods of stress, such as occurs when we change a job or move house. Berry & Webb (1983) found a strong correlation between self-reported levels of anxiety and 'sleep efficiency', and also discovered that the better the sleep attained by the participants in their study, the more positive were their moods on the following day.

Although the evidence is not conclusive, it is possible that sleep helps us recover from the psychological as well as the physiological exertions of our waking hours.

Studies of REM sleep deprivation

REM sleep has been of particular interest to researchers, largely because of its paradoxical nature. REM sleep might serve particular functions and much research has investigated this. As with sleep in general, the easiest way to address the role of REM sleep has been to deprive people of it and observe the consequences of the deprivation.

Dement (1960) had volunteers spend several nights at his sleep laboratory. They were allowed to sleep normally, but whenever they entered REM sleep they were woken up. A control group of volunteers was woken up the same number of times but only during NREM sleep. Compared with the control group, the REM-deprived group became increasingly irritable, aggressive and unable to concentrate on performing various tasks. As the experiment progressed, the REM-deprived group started to show *REM starvation*. After several nights they attempted to go into REM sleep as soon as they went to sleep, and it became increasingly difficult to wake them when they did manage to enter REM sleep.

On the first night, Dement had to wake the REM- deprived sleepers an average of 12 times each, but by the seventh night they had to be woken an average of 26 times, suggesting that the need for REM sleep was steadily increasing. Similarly, Borbely (1986) found that a REM sleep-deprived individual made 31 attempts to enter REM on the first night, 51 attempts on the second, and over 60 on the third!

When people are allowed to sleep normally after REM sleep deprivation most, but not all, show a REM *rebound effect* (they spend longer in REM sleep than is usually the case). This suggests that we try to make up for 'lost' REM sleep time, although firm conclusions cannot be drawn since the rebound effect is *not* observed in everyone. In general, the evidence suggests that we can adjust to REM sleep deprivation in much the same way that we can adjust to not eating for several days if necessary (Webb, 1975). REM sleep seems to be necessary, then, though depriving people of it does not appear to be psychologically harmful.

Box 2.6 *REM sleep, anxiety and alcohol*

Some researchers have looked at the effects of REM sleep deprivation on the reduction of anxiety. Greenberg *et al.* (1972) had participants watch a film of a circumcision rite performed without anaesthetic. On first viewing, the film elicits a high level of anxiety which gradually subsides on repeated viewing. However, the researchers found that people deprived of REM sleep did not show a reduction in their anxiety when they viewed the film on subsequent occasions. This suggests that REM sleep may, at least partly, act to reduce the anxiety of events that have occurred during the waking day.

Alcohol (see Chapter 5) suppresses REM sleep without affecting NREM sleep. When heavy alcohol users abstain, a REM rebound effect occurs. The effect can be very disturbing and the sharp increase in dreaming often leads to a resumption of heavy drinking. With severe alcohol abuse, a kind of REM rebound effect may occur during the waking hours. This manifests itself as the disturbing hallucinations experienced during alcohol withdrawal (Greenberg & Pearlman, 1967).

As noted earlier, the evidence generally suggests that there are few harmful effects following REM sleep deprivation. Indeed, according to Dement (1974), research:

'has failed to prove substantial ill-effects result from even prolonged selective REM deprivation'.

Whilst this may be true, the occurrence of the REM rebound effect, and the fact that REM-deprived sleepers try to enter REM sleep more and more over the course of time, suggests that REM sleep may serve important functions.

Restoration theories of REM sleep function

According to Oswald (1966), REM sleep is related to brain 'restoration' and growth. Studies have shown a greater rate of *protein synthesis* during REM sleep than in NREM sleep, and protein synthesis may serve as 'an organic basis for new developments in the personality' (Rossi, 1973). However, whether REM sleep causes increased protein synthesis or increased protein synthesis is the result of the increased activity of nerve cells that occurs during REM sleep, is less clear.

REM sleep does, however, differ over the lifespan and accounts for around 50 per cent of the total sleep time (TST) of a newborn baby as compared with only 20 per cent of the TST of an adult (see Figure 1.4). Indeed, in almost every mammalian species, adults sleep less than infants and spend less time in REM sleep as they get older. REM sleep may, therefore, promote the protein synthesis necessary for cell manufacture and growth, essential to the developing nervous system's maturation. The decline observed in adulthood may reflect a decrease in the rate of development of the brain's information processing capabilities.

REM sleep deprivation has the effect, in non-humans at least, of impairing learning. Bloch (1976) has shown that REM sleep increases when non-humans are given training on a new task and that this increase is greatest during the steepest part of the learning curve. Perhaps, then, the protein synthesis that occurs during REM sleep is a contributory factor in the formation of long-term memories. In humans, the consequence of a massive 'insult' to the brain by, for example, a drug overdose, results in an increase in the amount of time spent in REM sleep, as though some attempt was being made to repair the damage done.

However, even those who support the restoration theory of REM sleep function accept that REM sleep uses a substantial amount of energy (such as increased blood flow to the brain). Such activity would actually *prevent* high levels of protein synthesis. Researchers are still trying to reconcile these contradictory observations.

Some other theories of REM sleep function

Memory consolidation theory

REM sleep may stimulate neural tissue and consolidate information in memory. Empson & Clarke's (1970) participants heard unusual phrases before bedtime and were given a memory test about them the next morning. Those deprived of REM sleep remembered less than those woken the same number of times during the night but from other stages of sleep. This finding has been replicated on a number of occasions using various material (e.g. Tilley & Empson, 1978), although we should note that there is no evidence to suggest that *hypnopaedia* – learning whilst we are asleep – takes place (Rubin, 1968).

As noted in Chapter 1, REM sleep occurs in all mammals except the spiny anteater and dolphin, but not in non-humans such as fish, whose behaviour is less influenced by learning. It was also noted that the proportion of time spent in REM sleep declines with increasing age when, possibly, the need to consolidate memories is of less importance. The evidence concerning memory consolidation during REM sleep is mounting, and it seems likely that memory consolidation is an important function of REM sleep.

The sentinel theory

The observation that EEG activity resembles the patterns of activity observed during waking, and that short periods of wakefulness sometimes occur at the *end* of REM sleep, led Snyder (cited in Borbely, 1986) to suggest that REM sleep serves the function of allowing animals to check their surroundings periodically for signs of danger. Snyder sees the end of REM acting as a *sentinel* (or look-out) to ensure that animals are free from danger. Whilst this is an interesting suggestion, its main weakness lies in the fact that it sees only the *end* of REM sleep as serving any function. The time spent in REM sleep presumably serves no function at all. It is unlikely that many sleep researchers would agree with this.

The oculomotor system maintenance theory

Some researchers who might agree with Snyder are those who subscribe to the oculomotor system maintenance theory of REM sleep function. According to this, the function of REM sleep is to keep the eye muscles toned up. About once every 90 minutes during sleep, the eye muscles are given some exercise to keep them in trim. Although this theory may be tongue-in-cheek, it highlights one important point about theories of sleep function, namely that they are difficult to test and therefore falsify (as noted earlier, evolutionary theories of sleep seem to be capable of accommodating all of the findings concerning sleep patterns). It is difficult to see how Snyder's theory and the oculomotor system maintenance theory could be tested.

The physiology of sleep

Chapter 1 suggested that external cues are not of primary importance as far as the sleep-waking cycle is concerned. However, external cues do play a role. When night falls, the eyes inform the *supra-chiasmatic nucleus* (SN) and, via a neural pathway travelling through the hypothalamus, the *pineal gland*. As noted in Chapter 1, the pineal gland secretes melatonin. Melatonin influences neurons that produce serotonin, which is concentrated in the *raphe nuclei*. Serotonin is then released and acts on the *reticular activating system* (RAS).

Box 2.7   *Melatonin – the hormone of darkness*

Because melatonin is produced mainly at night, it has been called the hormone of darkness. In 1995, a synthetic version of melatonin was produced and marketed in America as a way of overcoming insomnia and jet lag (and, incidentally, as a rejuvenating substance). Although currently banned in the UK, because not enough is known about its effects, it has been used with blind people to resynchronise the biological clock by producing shifts of its timing, an effect probably mediated by the melatonin receptors in the suprachiasmatic nucleus (Minors, 1997).

It has long been known that the RAS is involved in consciousness. Moruzzi & Magoun (1949), for example, showed that stimulation of the RAS caused a slumbering cat to awaken, whereas destruction of the RAS caused a permanent coma. Jouvet (1967) showed that destruction of the raphe nuclei produces sleeplessness and, on the basis of the finding that serotonin is concentrated in this brain structure, he concluded that serotonin must play a role in the induction of sleep. Since serotonin is a *monoamine* neurotransmitter, Jouvet advanced his *monoamine hypothesis of sleep*.

Jouvet discovered that *paracholorophenylalanine* (PCPA), a substance which inhibits serotonin synthesis, prevents sleep.

However, if its effects are reversed (by means of *5-hydroxytrypto-phan*) then sleep is reinstated. This suggests that whilst serotonin may not play the role in the induction of sleep, it certainly plays a role. Other experiments conducted by Jouvet showed that destruction of the *locus coeruleus* (a small patch of dark cells located in the pons) caused REM sleep to disappear completely, suggesting that the pons plays a role in the regulation of REM sleep. Moreover, if neurons in a different part of the pons were destroyed, REM sleep remained but muscle tension (which is ordinarily absent during REM sleep) was *maintained*. This resulted in a cat moving around during REM sleep, even though it was completely unconscious.

For reasons that are not well understood, the inhibitory processes normally operating during REM sleep do not operate in some people (and this is called *REM behaviour disorder*). Sufferers may 'thrash violently about, leap out of bed, and may even attack their partners' (Chase & Morales, 1990). As mentioned in Chapter 1, dreaming is correlated with REM sleep and, presumably, being paralysed during REM sleep serves the useful biological function of preventing us from acting out dreams. Quite possibly, the cat described above was acting out a dream. 'Sleepwalking', then, cannot occur during REM sleep because the body's musculature is in a state of virtual paralysis. The stage in which it does occur is identified in Box 3.1 (see page 39).

The locus coeruleus produces *noradrenaline* and *acetylcholine*. Jouvet proposed that these were responsible for the onset of REM sleep and the associated loss of muscle tone. The fact that *carbachol*, a chemical which imitates acetylcholine's action but for a longer time, results in much longer periods of REM sleep, supports this view. Moreover, *scopolamine*, a substance which *inhibits* acetylcholine's action, leads to a dramatic *delay* in the onset of REM sleep.

Jouvet (1983) believes that sleep cycles occur as a result of the relationship between the raphe nuclei and locus coeruleus. The raphe nuclei are believed to initiate sleep (by acting on the RAS). Thereafter, interactions between the raphe nuclei and the locus coeruleus generate the NREM-REM sleep cycle. When one structure overcomes the other, wakefulness occurs.

The picture is undoubtedly more complicated than has been painted. For example, stimulation of the thalamus can induce sleep, and stimulation of other areas can prevent waking. The ventrolateral preoptic area of the hypothalamus, for example, has been found to provide direct input to neurons which contain *histamine*, *noradrenaline* and *serotonin*. This area might serve as an 'off-switch' for the brain and allow the simultaneous deactivation of all arousal systems. Nonetheless, the view that sleep is a passive process can certainly be dismissed. Both sleeping and waking must be the result of complex interactions between various brain structures.

Conclusions

This chapter has looked at theories of the functions of sleep in general and REM sleep in particular, and has examined what is known about the physiology of sleep. Presently, no theory is firmly supported by experimental evidence. For some, however, the question of why we sleep has a very simple answer. We sleep because we need to dream. If this is the case, another interesting question arises, concerning the function of dreaming. This question is addressed in Chapter 3.

Summary

- Sleep deprivation is used as a way of studying the functions of sleep. Controlled studies suggest a pattern of psychological reactions whose severity increases with increasing deprivation. After six nights without sleep, **sleep deprivation psychosis** occurs, although this disappears after a period of 'recovery sleep' (which need not last as long as the deprivation). There is little evidence that physical harm follows sleep deprivation.

- The evidence does not, however, imply that sleep has no value. Long-term sleep deprivation in rats fatally impairs the ability to regulate their own heat. Case studies of humans, who lose sleep as a result of brain damage, also indicate that long-term deprivation is fatal.

- Theories of sleep function attempt to explain the undeniable need for sleep. Meddis's **evolutionary theory** proposes that sleep time is related to an animal's metabolic rate, method of obtaining food and exposure to predators. Animals that have a high metabolic rate, gather food in the open, and are preyed upon, have little sleep.

- Webb's **hibernation theory** proposes that because natural selection would favour an animal that kept itself out of danger, sleep has survival value. In the evolutionary past of humans, sleeping at night would have reduced the risk of predation/accidents and conserved energy that would have been wasted spent hunting.

- Some evolutionary theorists argue that preyed-upon species sleep for short periods because of the constant threat of predation. Others argue that such species sleep longer to avoid predation. This account of different sleep times is non-falsifiable.

- **Restoration theories** propose that sleep restores depleted energy levels, eliminates waste products from the muscles, repairs cells and recovers lost physical abilities. Stage 4 sleep, strongly suspected of being involved in the growth process, increases after excessive physical exertion. Reduced Stage 4 sleep in the elderly may reflect a reduction in the need for growth hormone. Deprivation of Stage 4 sleep produces fibrositis-like symptoms in healthy people. All of these findings are consistent with the view that sleep serves a restorative function.

- Sleep, especially REM sleep, may also serve a psychological restorative function. Deprivation of REM sleep results in irritability, aggressiveness and the inability to concentrate. People deprived of REM sleep also show REM starvation and try to enter REM as soon as they return to sleep. Most people also show a 'rebound effect' following deprivation of REM sleep, and spend longer in that stage.

- REM sleep appears to be necessary, but being deprived of it does not appear to be psychologically harmful. It may be involved in brain restoration and growth, since more protein synthesis occurs in it than in NREM sleep. Because REM sleep decreases with age, it may promote maturation of the developing nervous system and increase the brain's information processing capabilities.

- REM sleep in non-humans increases during learning, especially in the steepest part of the learning curve, and so may be involved in long-term memory formation and consolidation. Studies using humans also point to a role in memory consolidation. However, the fact that increased blood flow to the brain during REM would actually prevent protein synthesis complicates the picture.

- Snyder's **sentinel theory** proposes that the brief awakenings which sometimes occur at the end of a period of REM sleep allow an animal periodically to monitor its environment for signs of danger. However, this function only concerns the end of REM sleep, not REM sleep itself.

- The **oculomotor system maintenance theory** proposes that REM sleep's function is to keep the eye muscles toned up. This tongue-in-cheek proposal highlights the lack of falsifiability apparent in many theories of sleep function.

- Several brain structures, including the supra-chiasmatic nucleus, raphe nuclei, hypothalamus, thalamus, pons, reticular activating system and locus coeruleus have been implicated in sleep. Melatonin, the hormone of darkness, is also involved, as are serotonin, noradrenaline, acetylcholine and histamine. Their roles are described in Jouvet's **monoamine hypothesis of sleep**.

- The view that sleep is a passive process is incorrect and both sleep and waking are the result of complex interactions occurring in the brain.

THE FUNCTIONS OF DREAMING

Introduction and overview

Dreams have long held a fascination for both laypeople and psychologists. Some cultures, for example, believe dreams to be the experiences of a world that is not available during the waking hours. Others see dreams as messages from the gods. Attempts to discover the meaning of dreams can be found in Babylonian records dating back to 5000 BC. The Bible, Talmud, Homer's *Iliad* and *Odyssey* all give accounts of the meaning of dreams. In the Bible, for example, dreams provided revelations. It was during a dream that Joseph learned there was to be a famine in Egypt. This chapter examines theories of the functions of dreaming. It begins, however, by looking at some of the basic findings obtained in this area.

Dreams: some basic findings

The pioneering research of Dement, Aserinsky and Kleitman which was described in Chapter 1 revealed much about dreaming. As noted, REM sleep is correlated with dreaming and so instead of relying on the sometimes hazy recall of a dreamer waking at the end of an eight-hour period of sleep, the waking of a dreamer during a REM sleep episode enabled a vivid account of a dream to be obtained.

Everyone shows the pattern of four to five REM sleep episodes per night. When woken from REM sleep, people report dreaming about 80 per cent of the time. Thus, people who claim that they don't dream really mean that they don't *remember* their dreams. There are wide individual differences in this, but those dreams that are remembered tend to be the ones occurring closest to waking up. People blind from birth also dream and have auditory dreams which are just as vivid and complex as the visual dreams of sighted people.

Dreams may be realistic and well organised, disorganised and uninformed, in black and white or colour, and emotional or unemotional. Although dreaming is most likely to occur in REM sleep, some occurs in NREM sleep. REM sleep dreams tend to be clear, highly detailed, full of vivid images and often reported as fantastic adventures with a clear plot. The eye movements that occur during REM sleep are sometimes correlated with a dream's content, but there is no one-to-one correspondence. NREM sleep dreams typically consist of fleeting images, lack detail, have vague plots and involve commonplace things.

Most dreams last as long as the events would in real life. Although time seems to expand and contract during a dream, 15 minutes of events occupies about 15 minutes of dream time. The actual content of a dream can be affected by pre-sleep events. For example, people deprived of water often dream of drinking (Bokert, 1970). Also, whilst the brain is relatively insensitive to outside sensory input, some external stimuli can either wake us up (see Box 1.5) or be incorporated into a dream. For example, Dement & Wolpert (1958) lightly sprayed cold water onto dreamers' faces. Compared with sleepers who were not sprayed, they were much more likely to dream about water, incorporating waterfalls, leaky roofs and, occasionally, being sprayed with water into their dreams.

Sex differences in dreaming have also been reported, with females typically dreaming about indoor settings and males about outdoor settings. Male dreams also tend to be more aggressive than female dreams. Contrary to popular belief, only a small proportion (one in ten in men and one in 30 in women) of dreams are clearly sexual in content (Hall & Van de Castle, 1966).

Box 3.1 *Lucid dreaming and sleepwalking*

Lucid dreamers report having dreams in which they knew they were dreaming and felt as if they were conscious during the dream. They can test their state of consciousness by attempting to perform impossible acts such as floating in the air. If the act can be performed, a lucid dream is occurring. Some lucid dreamers can control the course of events in a dream, and skilled dreamers can signal the onset of a lucid dream by moving their eyes in a way pre-arranged with the sleep researcher. Evidently, the technology now exists for all of us to become lucid dreamers (Hollington, 1995).

Contrary to popular belief, sleepwalking does not occur during REM sleep. It can't, since the musculature is in a state of virtual paralysis during REM sleep (see Chapter 2). As noted, the paralysis presumably prevents us from *acting out* a dream. When the part of the brain responsible for the inhibition of movement is damaged, a cat, for example, will move around during REM sleep. Perhaps, then, non-humans dream too! Sleepwalking occurs during the *deeper* stages of sleep when the musculature is not paralysed.

A great deal is known about the process of dreaming, but what possible functions does it serve? Some researchers believe that dreaming does not have a purpose. Kleitman (1963), for example, has suggested that:

> 'the low-grade cerebral activity that is dreaming may serve no significant function whatsoever'.

Others believe that dreams have important psychological functions.

Freud's theory of dream function

The first person to seriously consider the psychology of dreaming was Freud (1900) in *The Interpretation of Dreams*. Freud argued that a dream was a sort of 'psychic safety valve' which allowed a person to harmlessly discharge otherwise unacceptable and unconscious wishes and urges.

During the waking hours, these wishes and impulses are excluded from consciousness because of their unacceptable nature. During sleep, they are allowed to be expressed through the medium of dreams. As noted above, Freud saw them as relieving psychic tensions created during the day and gratifying unconscious desires. He also saw them as 'protecting sleep', by providing imagery that would keep disturbing and repressed thoughts out of consciousness.

Box 3.2 *Manifest and latent content*

Freud argued that unconscious desires are not gratified directly in a dream. What he called the *manifest content* of a dream (the dream as reported by the dreamer) is a censored and symbolic version of its deeper *latent content* (its actual meaning). According to Freud, a dream's meaning has to be 'disguised' because it consists of drives and wishes that would be threatening to us if they were expressed directly. Freud believed that the process of 'censorship' and 'symbolic transformation' accounted for the sometimes bizarre and highly illogical nature of dreams.

For Freud, dreams provide the most valuable insight into the motives that direct a person's behaviour, and he described a dream as 'the royal road to the unconscious'. The task of a dream analyst is to decode the manifest content of a dream into its latent content. Analysts call the objects that occur in a dream, and which camouflage its meaning, *symbols*. A gun, for example, might actually be a disguised representation of the penis. A person who dreamt of being *robbed* at gunpoint might be unconsciously expressing a wish to be sexually dominated. A person who dreamt of robbing someone at gunpoint might be unconsciously expressing a wish to be sexually dominant.

Freud believed that no matter how absurd a dream appeared to be to the dreamer, it always possessed meaning and logic. However, he did accept that there was a danger in translating the symbols, and warned that dreams had to be analysed in the context of a person's waking life as well as his/her associations with the dream's content: a broken candlestick may well represent a theme of impotence, but as Freud himself (a lover of cigars) famously remarked, 'sometimes a cigar is only a cigar'.

Table 3.1 *Sexual symbols in Freudian dream interpretation*

Symbols for the male genital organs

aeroplanes	fish	neckties	tools	weapons
bullets	hands	poles	trains	
feet	hoses	snakes	trees	
fire	knives	sticks	umbrellas	

Symbols for the female genital organs

bottles	caves	doors	ovens	ships
boxes	chests	hats	pockets	tunnels
cases	closets	jars	pots	

Symbols for sexual intercourse

climbing a ladder	entering a room
climbing a staircase	flying in an aeroplane
crossing a bridge	riding a horse
driving a car	riding a roller coaster
riding a lift	walking into a tunnel or down a hall

Symbols for the breasts

apples	peaches

It is, of course, possible that dreams have meaning and might reveal important issues and conflicts in a person's life. However, Freud's view that these issues and conflicts are always disguised has been criticised. For example, a person who is concerned with impotence is just as likely to dream about impotence as about broken candles. As Fisher & Greenberg (1977) have noted:

'there is no *rationale* for approaching a dream as if it were a container for a secret wish buried under layers of concealment'.

Freud's claim that part of the function of dreaming is to 'protect sleep' has also been challenged. Evidence suggests that disturbing events during the day tend to be followed by related disturbing dreams rather than 'protective imagery' (Foulkes, 1971; Cohen, 1973). Hall (1966), amongst others, has noted that the content of most dreams is consistent with a person's waking behaviour. Thus, there is little evidence to support the view that the primary function of dreaming is to act as a release for the expression of unacceptable impulses.

The major problem for Freud's theory of dream function is that the *interpretation* of a dream is not something that can be *objectively* achieved even if the interpreter is a trained psychoanalyst. According to Collee (1993):

> 'Metaphor is a notoriously ambiguous form of communication. You can suggest to me the meaning of having luminous feet, but the image will almost always mean something entirely different to you from what it means to me. So dreams end up in much the same category as tarot cards or tea leaves: just a system of images which the dream expert can manipulate to tell you exactly what they think you need to hear'.

Box 3.3 *Dreams and illness*

Another theory of dreams developed by Freud derives from practices in ancient Greece. At the Temple of Aesculapius, the physician Epidaurus administered drugs to people who, having slept and dreamt, then told him about their dreams. On the basis of the descriptions provided, Epidaurus was able to tell them the nature of their illness. Like the ancient Greeks, Freud believed that dreams were the body's way of telling us about physical illness. Psychoanalytic interest lies in the finding that dreams may precipitate illness or contribute to the distress of illness (Le Fanu, 1994).

A 'problem-solving' theory of dreaming

Webb & Cartwright (1978) see dreams as a way of dealing with problems relating to work, sex, health, relationships and so on that occur during the waking hours. Cartwright (1978) argues that whatever is symbolised in a dream is the dream's true meaning and, unlike Freud, she sees no reason to distinguish between a dream's manifest and latent content. Like Freud, however, Cartwright makes much use of the role of metaphor in dreaming.

Cartwright suggests that a person dreaming of, say, being buried beneath an avalanche whilst carrying several books might be worried about being 'snowed under' with work. Dreaming of a colleague trying to stab you in the neck might indicate that the colleague is a 'pain in the neck'. Cartwright has claimed support for her theory from several studies. In one, participants were presented with common problems which needed solving. Those allowed to sleep uninterrupted generated far more realistic solutions than those deprived of REM sleep.

Additionally, Hartmann (1973) has shown that people experiencing interpersonal or occupational problems enter REM sleep earlier and spend longer in it than people without such problems. For Cartwright, then, dreams are a way of identifying and dealing with many of life's problems. As she has noted, people going through crises need the support of friends and family, a little bit of luck and 'a good dream system'.

'Reprogramming' theories of dreaming

According to Evans (1984), the brain needs to periodically shut itself off from sensory input in order to process and assimilate new information and update information already stored. This shutting off is REM sleep, during which the brain 'mentally reprograms' its memory systems. The dreams we experience are the brain's attempts at interpreting this updating.

Support for this theory has been claimed from studies which show that REM sleep increases following activities requiring intense or unusual mental activity (such as performing complex and frustrating tasks). For example, Herman & Roffwarg (1983) had participants spend the waking day wearing distorting lenses that made the visual world appear upside down. After this experience, which demands considerable mental effort, participants spent longer than usual in REM sleep. Evans' theory would explain this in terms of the brain needing to spend a longer period of time 'off-line', processing and assimilating the experience. The finding that older people spend shorter periods of time dreaming is also consistent with Evans' theory: presumably, the older we get, the less need there is to reprogram our memory systems.

An alternative 'reprogramming' theory has been offered by Foulkes (1985). Like some other sleep researchers, Foulkes argues that dreams occur as a result of spontaneous activity in the nervous system. Foulkes argues that this activity can be related to our cognitive processes. The activation that occurs in the brain may well be spontaneous and random, but our cognitive systems are definitely *not* random. According to Foulkes, these systems, which we use in interpreting new experiences, themselves try to interpret the brain activity that occurs during REM sleep. Because of the structure imposed on the activation by our cognitive systems, dreams consist of events that generally occur in a way that makes at least some sense.

Box 3.4 *Foulkes' functions of dreams*

For Foulkes, dreams have at least four functions. First, most dreams usually refer to and reflect the memories and knowledge of the dreamer. One function might therefore be to relate *newly* acquired knowledge to one's own self-consciousness. Second, a dream might help integrate and combine specific knowledge and experiences acquired through the various senses with more general knowledge acquired in the past. Third, dreams often contain events that could, or might, have happened to us, but did not. By dreaming about something that has not yet occurred, but which might, a dream may serve the function of programming us to be prepared for dealing with new, unexpected events. Finally, since dreams are shaped by basic cognitive systems, they may reveal important information about the nature of our cognitive processes.

A third 'reprogramming' theory, which is a variation of the second function of dreams proposed by Foulkes, has been proposed by Koukkou & Lehman (1980). They argue that during a dream we combine ideas and strategies of thinking which originated in childhood with recently acquired relevant information. For them, a dream is a restructuring and reinterpretation of data already stored in memory.

Like some other theorists, Koukkou and Lehman clearly see dreams as being *meaningful*. However, some researchers have challenged this view, arguing that dreams are a meaningless consequence of brain activity during sleep.

Hobson and McCarley's 'activation-synthesis' theory

One of the best known biopsychological theories of dream function is the 'activation-synthesis' theory proposed by Hobson & McCarley (1977). Hobson (1989) showed that in cats, certain neurons deep within the brain fire in a seemingly random manner during REM sleep. The firing of these neurons *activates* adjacent neurons which are involved in the control of eye movements, gaze, balance, posture and activities such as running and walking.

As noted in Chapter 2, most body movements are inhibited during REM sleep. However, signals are still sent to the parts of the cerebral cortex responsible for visual information processing and voluntary actions when we are awake. Thus, although the body is not moving, the brain receives signals which suggest that it is. In an attempt to make sense of this contradiction, the brain, drawing on memory and other stored information, attempts to *synthesise* the random bursts of neural activity. The result of its efforts is the dream we experience.

The process of synthesis results in the brain imposing some order on the chaotic events caused by the firing of neurons, but it cannot do this in a particularly sophisticated way. This would explain why dreams often comprise shifting and fragmentary images. As Hobson & McCarley (1977) have noted, the dream itself is the brain's effort 'to make the best out of a bad job'. For Hobson and McCarley, then, dream content is the by-product of the random stimulation of nerve cells rather than the unconscious wishes suggested by Freud. Whereas Freud saw dreams as 'the royal road to the unconscious', Hobson and McCarley see them as inherently random and meaningless.

Box 3.5 *Giant cells and 'synaptic ammunition'*

Hobson (1988) has also offered an explanation of why the brain is periodically activated during the sleep cycle. He argues that *giant cells*, which are found in the reticular activating system and the pons, are responsible for the onset of REM sleep and sensitive to *acetylcholine*. When acetylcholine is available, the giant cells fire in an unrestrained way, but when no more is available they stop.

Hobson uses the analogy of a machine gun which can fire bullets very quickly when the cartridge is full, but can do nothing once it has emptied. The end of REM sleep occurs because there is no more 'synaptic ammunition'. When synaptic ammunition, in the form of acetylcholine, becomes available again, the giant cells start firing and another period of REM sleep begins.

Hobson and McCarley's theory has attracted considerable support because of its apparent explanatory power. For example, our strong tendency to dream about events that have occurred during the day presumably occurs because the most current neural activity of the cortex is that which represents the concerns or events of the day. Commonly experienced dreams about falling are, presumably, the brain attempting to interpret activity in the neurons involved in balance, whilst dreams about floating are the brain's attempt to interpret neural activity in the inner ear.

Activation-synthesis theory is also capable of explaining why we do not experience smells and tastes during a dream. This is because the neurons responsible are not stimulated during REM sleep. Our inability to remember dreams occurs because the neurons in the cortex that control the storage of new memories are turned 'off'. Finally, evidence concerning the role of acetylcholine in REM sleep is also consistent with Hobson and McCarley's theory (see page 33).

Yet whilst Hobson believes that activation synthesis theory has 'opened the door to the molecular biology of sleep' (and closed it on the Freudian approach to dreaming: Bianchi, 1992), it has not escaped criticism. According to Foulkes (1985), the content of dreams is influenced by our waking experiences and, therefore, dreams cannot be as random and psychologically meaningless as Hobson and McCarley suggest.

In response to this, Hobson (1988) has accepted that:

'the brain is so inexorably bent upon the quest for meaning that it attributes and even creates meaning when there is little or none in the data it is asked to process'.

However, although dreams might contain 'unique stylistic psychological features and concerns' which provide us with insights into our 'life strategies' and, perhaps, ways of coping, the activation synthesis theory most definitely sees dreams as the result of brain stem activities rather than unconscious wishes.

Crick and Mitchison's 'reverse learning' theory of dreams

According to Crick & Mitchison (1983), the function of dreaming is to enable the brain to get rid of information it doesn't need by weakening undesirable synaptic connections and erasing 'inappropriate modes of brain activity' which have been produced either by the physical growth of brain cells or experience. Crick and Mitchison propose that during REM sleep, random firing of neurons in the brain sets off undesirable connections, such as hallucinations and fantasies, that have overloaded the cortex. By 'flushing out' the excessive accumulation of 'parasitic information', more space is made available in memory for useful information. 'We dream in order to forget', they write, and call this process *reverse learning* or *unlearning*.

Crick and Mitchison argue that their theory is supported by the finding that all mammals except the spiny anteater and dolphin have REM sleep (when dreaming is most likely to occur). Both of these mammals have an abnormally large cortex for their size, which Crick and Mitchison believe is because they do not dream. Consequently, they need an especially large cortex to accommodate all the useless information they have accumulated, which cannot be disposed of.

For Crick and Mitchison, then, dreams serve a biologically useful process in that they keep the nervous system functioning effectively. However, a dream's content is an accidental result that does not lend itself to meaningful interpretation. Indeed, remembering dreams is *bad* for us because we are storing again the very information we were trying to dispose of!

Box 3.6 *Dreams and creativity*

One problem for theories which see dreams as meaningless events is that history is littered with stories of discoveries or creations that came to people during a dream. The chemist August Kekulé once dreamed of six snakes chasing each other in such a way that the snake in front was biting the snake behind. From this, he deduced the structure of the benzene ring. Robert Louis Stevenson is said to have dreamed the plot of *Dr Jekyll and Mr Hyde*. His wife told him he was talking in his sleep. Angrily, he replied: 'What did you wake me for? I was dreaming a fine wee bogy tale'.

All theories of dreaming have difficulty in accounting for the observation that something very much like REM sleep occurs in the developing foetus. What unconscious wishes could a developing foetus have? What 'parasitic information' could a foetus be getting rid of? According to Jouvet (1983), the only possible explanation is that REM sleep serves to program processes in the brain necessary for the development and maintenance of genetically determined functions, such as instincts. This theory suggests that REM sleep generates a sensory activity pattern in the brain – the dream – that is independent of the external world (Borbely, 1986). Jouvet sees the activity of nerve cells that occurs in REM sleep as representing a code which is capable of activating information stored in the genes. This inborn instinctive behaviour is 'practiced' during REM sleep. After birth, it is combined with acquired or learned information.

Box 3.7 *To sleep, perchance to experience amygdalocortical activation and prefrontal deactivation?*

Maquet *et al.* (cited in Highfield, 1996c) persuaded participants connected to an EEG machine to sleep in a PET scanner, their heads pinned in place by a special face mask. The PET scans confirmed the existence of activity in the pons during REM sleep, and also indicated activity in the left thalamus, which receives signals from the brainstem. Of most interest, though, was the activity in the left and right amygdalas. Since one role of these structures is the formation and consolidation of memories of emotional experience, it seems likely that REM sleep is, as theorists like Evans (1984) have proposed, involved in memory processing.

Maquet *et al.* also found reduced activity in the prefrontal cortex, which is involved in self-awareness and the planning of behaviour. They argue that the 'dampening down' of this area may prevent us from realising that a dream is actually unreal, and may be why dreams appear real. The prefrontal cortex's reduced activity may also explain the distortions in time that occur in a dream and the forgetting of a dream after waking (see Figure 3.1).

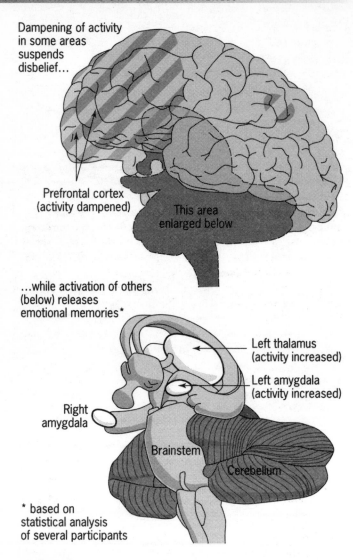

Dampening of activity in some areas suspends disbelief...

Prefrontal cortex (activity dampened)

This area enlarged below

...while activation of others (below) releases emotional memories*

Left thalamus (activity increased)

Left amygdala (activity increased)

Right amygdala

Brainstem

Cerebellum

* based on statistical analysis of several participants

Figure 3.1 *Maquet* et al.*'s findings*
(The Telegraph Group Limited, London, 1996)

Conclusions

This chapter has reviewed several theories of the function of dreaming. These see dreams as being meaningful or meaningless. Because they are difficult to test, none can be disqualified or accepted. A final answer to the question posed at the beginning of the chapter is not, at present, available. As Collee (1993) has observed:

> 'There is a danger in thinking about the body in teleologial terms – imagining that everything has a function, whereas we know that a lot of what happens is accidental. Yawning is one example of such accidents of nature, seeming to be just the useless by-product of various important respiratory reflexes. Dreams might have no function at all or they might have a heap of different functions all jumbled together so that one obscures the other. They might just be the films your brain plays to entertain itself while it is sleeping.'

Summary

- The correlation between REM sleep and dreaming enables dreams to be studied scientifically. Everyone experiences four to five episodes of REM sleep per night, and when woken from it report dreaming 80 per cent of the time. Some dreams occur in NREM sleep, but there are important differences in quality and content between them and REM sleep dreams.
- Events in dreams tend to last as long as they would in real life, and a dream's content can be affected by pre-sleep events and events occurring during REM sleep. There are differences in men and women's dreams, although we have fewer dreams about sex than is commonly believed.
- **Lucid dreamers** are aware that they are having a dream and can sometimes control the events that occur in it. Sleepwalking cannot occur in REM sleep since the musculature is virtually paralysed. Sleepwalking must occur in stages of sleep other than REM sleep.
- According to Freud, a dream is a 'safety valve' which allows us to harmlessly discharge otherwise unacceptable and

unconscious urges and wishes. The dream reported by the dreamer (its **manifest content**) is a censored and symbolic version of its actual meaning (**latent content**).

- Freud's theory has been widely criticised. For example, there is little evidence to support his view that the function of dreaming is to 'protect sleep', since disturbing events during the day tend to be followed by related disturbing dreams rather than 'protective imagery'. The non-falsifiability of dream interpretation is the theory's major weakness.

- Dreams have also been proposed as ways of solving problems. Evidence suggests that people experiencing interpersonal/occupational problems enter REM sleep earlier and spend longer in it than those without such problems.

- Evans' **reprogramming theory** suggests that dreams are the brain's attempt at interpreting the processing and assimilation of new information, and updating information already stored. Support for this comes from the finding that REM sleep time increases following activities requiring intense/unusual mental activity.

- Foulkes' **reprogramming theory** claims that a dream is an attempt to interpret the random and spontaneous brain activity that occurs in REM sleep. A dream usually makes some sense because our cognitive system imposes its structure on this otherwise meaningless activity. Dreams help integrate specific knowledge and experiences with more general knowledge acquired in the past, and can aid in preparing us for new, unexpected events. They may do this by restructuring data stored in memory in the light of new experiences.

- **Activation-synthesis theory** suggests that dreams are essentially meaningless and reflect the brain's unsophisticated attempt to make sense of the electrical activity that occurs in REM sleep. A dream occurs when giant cells in the reticular activating system and the pons are activated by acetylcholine. When acetylcholine is no longer available, the giant cells' activity ceases and REM sleep ends.

- Activation–synthesis theory has much apparent explanatory power. For example, activity in the neurons involved in balance explain dreams about falling, whilst dreams about floating are the brain's attempt to interpret neuronal activity in the inner ear. However, if dreams are influenced by our waking experiences, then dreaming cannot be completely random and meaningless.

- Crick and Mitchison's **reverse learning theory** proposes that dreams enable the brain to erase information that is no longer needed by weakening certain synaptic connections. Random firing of neurons sets off undesirable connections, such as hallucinations and fantasies, that have overloaded the cortex. The 'flushing out' of 'parasitic information' creates more space in memory for useful information.

- Crick and Mitchison see the absence of REM sleep in the spiny anteater and dolphin as consistent with their theory, since both of these have abnormally large cortexes for their size. An abnormally large cortex would be needed if there were no way of removing useless information.

- Historical accounts of discoveries and creations coming to people during dreams are difficult for reverse learning theory to explain. The observation of REM-like sleep in the developing foetus poses problems for all theories of dreaming, although an attempt to account for this phenomenon has been offered by Jouvet.

HYPNOSIS AND
HYPNOTIC PHENOMENA

4 Introduction and overview

Like dreaming, hypnosis has long been of fascination to both laypeople and psychologists. This chapter reviews what is known about hypnosis and hypnotic phenomena. It begins by briefly looking at the history of hypnosis and, after describing the induction of a hypnotic state, considers some of its major characteristics. It then looks at two major theories of hypnosis before examining some practical applications of hypnosis and the issue of hypnosis and behaviour control.

A brief history of hypnosis

Serious scientific interest in hypnosis can be traced to 1784, when King Louis XVI of France established a committee to investigate the work of Franz Anton Mesmer. Like some present-day physicists, Mesmer believed that the universe was connected by a mysterious form of 'magnetism'. He also believed that human beings could be drawn to one another by a process called *animal magnetism*.

Box 4.1 *Animal magnetism*

According to Mesmer, illnesses were caused by imbalances in the body's own magnetic fields. Since he considered himself to possess a very large amount of 'magnetic fluid', Mesmer reasoned that by rechannelling his own magnetism he could cure the sick, because their 'magnetic fluxes' would be restored. *Mesmerism*, the treatment devised by Mesmer, was unusual. In a darkened room, patients, who held iron bars, were seated around wooden barrels filled with water, ground glass and iron filings. With soft music playing in the background Mesmer, dressed in a lilac taffeta robe, would walk around the room and occasionally tap the patients with his bar. Often, they would suffer convulsions and enter a trance-like state. When this occurred, Mesmer's assistants removed them to a mattress-lined room so they would not harm themselves.

Using his techniques, Mesmer apparently cured some minor ailments. However, Louis XVI's committee did not believe that 'animal magnetism' was responsible. In its view, cures probably occurred through 'aroused imagination' or what would today be called the *placebo effect*. Although the committee's conclusions led to a decline of interest in Mesmer, 'Mesmerism' and 'animal magnetism', physicians remained interested in the possibility that similar techniques had a use, especially to reduce pain during surgery.

In 1842, Long, an American surgeon, operated on an etherised patient, the first instance of anaesthesia being used in medicine. In the same year, Ward, a British physician, reported that he had amputated a man's leg without causing any discomfort and without anything other than 'hypnosis' (a word coined by another British physician, Braid, and taken from the Greek *hypnos* meaning 'sleep'). Between 1845 and 1851, Eskdale performed many operations in India using hypnosis as his only anaesthetic. The technique's success was indicated by the fact that Eskdale's patients appeared to show no sign of suffering during their operations, and no apparent memory for having been in pain.

Inducing a hypnotic state

There are several ways of inducing a 'hypnotic state', the only requirement of any of them being that a person understands hypnosis will take place. Typically, the individual is asked to stare upwards and focus attention on a 'target' such as a small light or a spot on the wall. As attention is focused, the hypnotist makes suggestions of relaxation, tiredness and sleepiness. Contrary to popular belief, hypnotised people are *not* asleep. Although the eyes are closed, EEG recordings do not show the patterns characteristic of the stages of sleep (see Chapter 1), even though rapid eye movements may be seen beneath the closed eyelids.

The hypnotist may also suggest that the arms and legs feel heavy (an *ideomotor* suggestion) or warm (an *ideosensory* suggestion). The *expectation* of bodily changes can be sufficient to produce them. The suggestions probably reduce activity in the sympathetic branch of the autonomic nervous system (ANS) and help bring about the relaxed state. If the eyes are still open after ten minutes, the hypnotist will suggest they be closed. After further suggestions of relaxation, hypnotic tests are administered (Heap, 1996).

Characteristics of the hypnotic state

Several characteristics are associated with the hypnotic state, some or all of which may be apparent in a hypnotised person. *Suspension of planning* is a loss of ability to initiate actions. Thus, hypnotised people sit quietly and show little or no activity. If, however, an activity is suggested, the suggestion is responded to. Another characteristic is a *distortion in information processing*. Hypnotised people tend to accept inconsistencies or incongruities that would ordinarily be noticed. A *narrowing of attention* also occurs and results in less awareness of sensory information. For example, a person told to listen to only the hypnotist's voice will apparently hear no other voices. This is interesting because it has been shown that there is no reduction in sensory sensitivity and information is *still* analysed by the brain (see Box 4.2).

Hypnotised people will also respond to suggestions that their arms are becoming lighter and will rise, or that their hands are becoming 'attracted' to one another. As well as initiating movements, suggestion can inhibit it. A person told that the arm is 'rigid' will report being unable to bend it at all or only with extreme difficulty. Feelings and perceptions suggested by the hypnotist are also experienced, even if they are not consistent with actual external conditions. For example, a person told that the bottle beneath his or her nose contains water may report smelling nothing, even though it contains ammonia in the concentration found in household bleach.

Box 4.2 *Sensory information processing and hypnosis*

In the Ponzo illusion (a), the two parallel horizontal lines are the same length, but the top one looks longer than the bottom one. If, through hypnotic suggestion, the slanted lines are made to 'disappear', participants still report the top line as looking longer (Miller *et al.*, 1973). This shows that the visual system continues to process sensory information during hypnosis. If this were not the case, the lines would be perceived as being equal in length, as in (b).

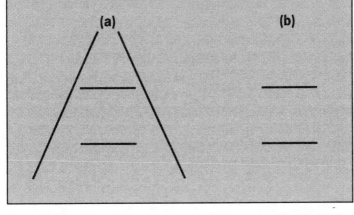

(a)　　　　　　　　　　　**(b)**

In *post-hypnotic amnesia*, the hypnotist may instruct the hypnotised individual to forget all that has occurred during the session. On 'awakening', the person may have no knowledge of the session and may not even be aware that hypnosis has occurred. When hypnotised again, however, recall of the original session's events usually occurs.

Box 4.3 *Positive and negative hallucinations*

Other perceptual distortions include the uncritical acceptance of hallucinated experiences. For example, hypnotised people may talk to an imaginary person they are told is sitting next to them without checking if this person is real. Responding to something that is not present is called a *positive hallucination*. Failing to respond to something that is present is called a *negative hallucination*.

In *post-hypnotic suggestion*, a person is given an instruction during the session that, for instance, on hearing the word 'sleep' afterwards, he or she will fall into a deep sleep. Responses to post-hypnotic suggestions seem to occur even when a person has been instructed to forget that the suggestions have been made. Of particular interest is the finding that a person eliciting a post-hypnotic response will, in the absence of any reason for making it, attempt to justify it. For example, a person instructed to eat a banana whenever the hypnotist says a particular word may justify the behaviour by saying that he or she 'feels hungry'. Not surprisingly, post-hypnotic suggestion has been used with people who wish to stop smoking but have otherwise been unable to do so. Typically, a *hypnotherapist* will make the suggestion that a lighted cigarette tastes repulsive.

Individual differences in hypnotic susceptibility

Not everyone is susceptible to hypnosis (Bates 1993). Hilgard (1977) estimates that 5–10 per cent of people are highly *resistant* and about 15 per cent highly susceptible. The remaining 75–80 per cent fall somewhere between these two extremes. One device for measuring susceptibility is the *Stanford hypnotic susceptibility scale*. Many of the phenomena included in the scale have already been referred to above.

Box 4.4   *The Stanford hypnotic susceptibility scale*

1 **Arm lowering:** It is suggested to the participant that an outstretched arm is getting heavier and heavier. The arm should be gradually lowered.
2 **Moving hands apart:** The participant sits with arms outstretched in front. The suggestion is made that the hands are repelled from each other as if by magnets. This should lead to them moving part.

---

3 Mosquito hallucination: The suggestion is made to the participant that an annoying mosquito is buzzing around. This should lead to the participant trying to 'shoo' it away.

4 Taste hallucination: The participant should respond to the suggestion that a sweet substance and then a sour one is being tasted.

5 Arm rigidity: Following the suggestion that an arm held out straight is getting stiffer and stiffer, the participant should be unable to unbend it.

6 Dream: The participant is told to have a dream about hypnosis whilst remaining hypnotised. The contents of the dream should be released by the participant.

7 Age regression: The participant is told to imagine being at different school ages. For each of the ages selected, realistic handwriting specimens should be provided.

8 Arm immobilisation: Following the suggestion made by the hypnotist, the participant should be unable to lift an arm voluntarily.

9 Anosmia (loss of smell) to ammonia: Following suggestions made by the hypnotist, the participant should report being unable to smell household ammonia.

10 Hallucinated voice: The participant should answer questions raised by a hallucinated voice.

11 Negative visual hallucination: Following suggestions made by the hypnotist, the participant should report the inability to see one of three small coloured boxes.

12 Post-hypnotic amnesia: The participant should be unable to recall particular information after hypnosis until given a pre-arranged signal.

After induction of a hypnotic state, the first suggestion is made. If responded to, it is counted as 'present' and the second suggestion made. The procedure continues until a response is counted as 'absent'. Since the 12 suggestions are ordered in terms of difficulty, a person who does not respond to the first is unlikely to respond to the second, third, and so on.

Hypnotic susceptibility is not related to any particular personality type (Oakley *et al.*, 1996). However, several stable personality traits are correlated with hypnotic susceptibility. These include *absorption* (the tendency to become deeply absorbed in sensory and imaginative experiences), *expectancy* (people are not influenced by hypnotic suggestions if they do not expect to be, and those who do usually are and typically have very positive attitudes towards hypnosis) and *fantasy-proneness* (having frequent and vivid fantasies).

These observations do not, of course, indicate that such characteristics *cause* susceptibility to hypnosis (Kirsch & Council, 1992). Moreover, at least one of them ('absorption') is correlated with hypnotic susceptibility only when people expect to *undergo* hypnosis. In other contexts, the correlation is not obtained (Council *et al.*, 1986). As a general rule, though, a person who becomes deeply absorbed in activities, expects to be influenced by hypnotic suggestions (or 'shows the faith' – Baron, 1989), and has a rich, vivid and active fantasy life, is likely to be more susceptible to hypnotic suggestions.

Box 4.5 *The neuropsychophysiology of hypnosis*

The transition from a non-hypnotised to hypnotised state has been described as a shift from an analytical and sequential mode of processing to more imaginal and holistic processing (Oakley *et al.*, 1996). Crawford (1994) has shown that frontal and possibly left-biased hemispheric activation prior to hypnosis is followed by a more posterior and possibly right-biased activation during induction. Evidently, these patterns and the shifts between them are more marked in people susceptible to hypnosis (Oakley *et al.*, 1996).

The genuineness of hypnosis

According to Orne & Evans (1965), all the phenomena that can be produced under hypnosis can be produced without hypnosis. Spanos *et al.* (1983) have proposed that the essential difference between hypnotised and non-hypnotised people is that the former *believe* their responses are involuntary, whereas the latter *know they are pretending*. Although hypnotic phenomena seem to be genuine enough, the genuineness of at least some of them has been questioned.

As noted earlier, in post-hypnotic amnesia people act as though they cannot remember what happened during a hypnotic episode. Spanos *et al.* (1982) have explained this in terms of the suggestion not to recall information being an 'invitation' to refrain from attending to retrieval cues. However, when people are given a 'lie detector' test and led to believe that they will be found out if they do not tell the truth, recall of the hypnotic episode increases dramatically! (Coe & Yashinski, 1985). This, along with other findings, has led to the suggestion that hypnotic phenomena are not real but merely a clever act perpetrated by the hypnotist and the participant, the latter pretending to be 'under the influence'.

Several studies have investigated *trance logic*, the difference in performance between the hypnotised and those pretending to be hypnotised. Orne *et al.* (1968) hypnotised one group of participants and instructed a second to act as though they were hypnotised. Both groups were told that in the following 48 hours their right hand would touch their foreheads every time they heard the word 'experiment'. Later, participants encountered a secretary who said the word 'experiment' three times. Participants highly susceptible to hypnosis touched their foreheads an average of 70 per cent of the occasions on which the word was said. For the hypnotised participants the figure was 29.5 per cent. For those pretending to be hypnotised it was only 7.7 per cent. Kinnunen *et al.* (1995) have used skin conductance reaction (SCR), a crude but effective measure of deception, to investigate hypnosis. They found significantly higher SCRs for 'simulators' compared with hypnotised individuals.

Bowers (1976) has shown that participants who are told they cannot see a chair *will* bump into it if they are faking hypnosis, but will walk around it (just as a sleepwalker does) if they have been hypnotised. Other research indicates that hypnotic susceptibility peaks between nine and 12 years of age, decreases until the mid-30s, and then levels off (Hart & Hart, 1996). The finding that hypnotised and non-hypnotised individuals can be shown to differ behaviourally, and that there is no reason why hypnotic susceptibility should change over time if it is faked, suggests that hypnotic phenomena *may* be real.

A 'state' or 'special processes' theory of hypnosis

According to *state* or *special processes* theorists, hypnosis is a unique and altered state of consciousness. Hilgard's (1977) *neo-dissociation theory* proposed that hypnosis is the dissociation (or division) of consciousness into separate channels of mental activity. This division allows us to focus our attention on the hypnotist and, simultaneously, enables us to perceive other events peripherally (or 'subconsciously').

Box 4.6   *The hidden observer and the cold pressor test*

Central to Hilgard's theory is the *hidden observer* phenomenon. Hilgard (1973) told a male participant that deafness would be induced in him through hypnosis, but that he would be able to hear when a hand was placed on his shoulder. Although 'hypnotically deaf', he was asked to raise a forefinger if there was some part of him that could still hear. To Hilgard's surprise, and that of a watching audience, a forefinger rose.

Hilgard also explored the hidden observer phenomenon using the *cold pressor test* (CPT). In this, one or both forearms is plunged into circulating icy water and the participant is required to keep the forearm(s) submerged for as long as possible. Initially, the sensation is of coldness. After a few seconds, however, this turns to pain which cannot be tolerated by most people for longer than about 25 seconds. Hilgard found that when participants highly susceptible to hypnosis were told that they would feel no pain, they kept their forearm(s) submerged for an average of around 40 seconds.

Although hypnotised participants appear to be able to withstand pain in the CPT for longer than would ordinarily be the case, the hidden observer does not! Thus, when the hidden observer was asked to 'remain out of awareness' and write down ratings of pain on a ten-point scale, the ratings were significantly higher than those reported verbally by the participant. This finding is consistent with Hilgard's theory: the part of consciousness accepting and responding to the hypnotist's suggestions becomes dissociated from the pain whilst the hidden observer, which monitors everything that happens, remains aware of it. This could be explained in terms of neural inhibition preventing information transmission between the verbal system ('consciousness') and the brain's peripheral and motor systems. This might be the 'dissociation' Hilgard refers to.

Earlier, it was noted that hypnosis has a long history as an *analgesic* (or 'pain-reliever'). For example, as well as helping children withstand painful bone marrow transplants for cancer, hypnosis has been used in various surgical procedures including the removal of teeth, tonsils and breast tumours (Hart & Alden, 1994). Indeed, it has been argued that the analgesic effects of hypnosis are more powerful than those of drugs like morphine, and can even act to reduce the emotional upset that accompanies pain as well as the pain itself (Millar, 1996). Hilgard's findings suggest that hypnosis does not eliminate pain, but enables it to be tolerated better because there is no conscious awareness of it. Spanos (1991) uses the term *strategic enactment* to refer to the adoption of a strategy (such as mental distraction) which, if the analgesia occurs, can be attributed to hypnosis.

Box 4.7 *The analgesic properties of hypnosis*

Other ways of explaining the analgesic properties of hypnosis have been advanced. Hypnosis may relax people. By encouraging them to focus on pleasant images, they might be distracted from thoughts of pain. Relaxation itself might allow the brain to produce *endorphins* (natural painkillers). Whether hypnosis really does have analgesic properties has been the subject of much debate. According to Barber (1970), even if people do experience pain when hypnotised, they might not wish to report this for fear of causing offence! Whether people are simply *acting* as though they are anaesthetised was studied by Pattie (1937). He told participants that they would be unable to feel anything with one hand. They were instructed to cross their wrists as illustrated below.

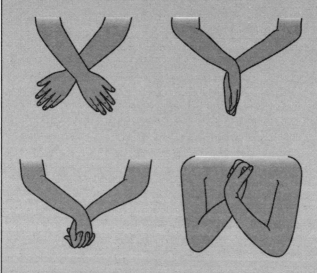

If you try this, and ask someone to touch one of your hands very rapidly, you'll find that it is difficult to determine which hand has been touched. Pattie showed that when he touched the fingers on both hands and asked participants to count the number of times they had been touched, they included touches made to the 'anaesthetised' hand (which should not have been counted if the hand really were anaesthetised). This suggests a difference between local anaesthesia and hypnotic anaesthesia. In the latter, a person behaves *as though* he or she is anaesthetised.

A 'non-state' theory of hypnosis

Barber (1979) takes a very different approach to Hilgard in explaining hypnotic phenomena. Barber argues that if hypnotic phenomena occur only when a person is hypnotised, it is difficult to see why the brain should have evolved in such a way that people *can* be hypnotised. For Barber, the functional analysis of a behavioural phenomenon usually points to a plausible reason for its occurrence. Thus, as far as Barber and other *non-state theorists* are concerned, hypnosis is *not* an altered state of consciousness.

Non-state theorists see hypnotised people as acting out a *social role*, which is defined by their own expectations and the situation in which they find themselves. The rules of the situation are governed by the hypnotist's direct instructions or indirectly implied by his or her words and actions (Wagstaff, 1991). In Barber's view, hypnosis is not special but people, and their imagination and ability to play roles, are.

Non-state theorists argue that hypnosis involves the *suspension of self-control*, a phenomenon which occurs when, say, we allow the actors in a film or the author of a book to lead us through some sort of fantasy. Certainly, the finding that 'suggestible' hypnotic participants have (amongst other things) vivid and absorbing imaginations, lends support to a non-state perspective and casts doubt on the claim that hypnosis is an altered state of consciousness.

Non-state theory is also supported by the finding that behaviours possible under hypnosis are also possible in non-hypnotic conditions. The 'human plank' trick, for example, in which a hypnotised person remains suspended from chairs placed at the back of the head and ankles, can be accomplished by most people in a normal waking state. Even Orne (1959), a leading researcher in the area, has acknowledged that the behaviour of non-hypnotised people occasionally fooled him:

'As a clinician who worked extensively with hypnosis, I never doubted it would be easy for me to recognise those who were, in

fact, simulating. It came as a complete surprise to find that [people] were able to deceive me'.

According to non-state theorists, the hidden observer phenomenon is simply a product of a *script* which is supplied by the hypnotist. Using the CPT, Spanos *et al.* (1983) told hypnotised participants that they would not experience any pain. Some were also given instructions similar to those used by Hilgard to elicit the hidden observer, whilst others were told that the hidden observer was *less* aware of things going on in and around their bodies. Compared with participants in whom the hidden observer was not elicited, the hidden observer reported more *or* less pain depending on the instructions that had been given.

Spanos *et al.* suggest that these findings reflect the playing of *two* roles rather than a division of consciousness. They argue that participants in Hilgard's experiment ignored the pain when told it would not be perceived and switched attention to it when the hidden observer was requested. Rather than being a part of consciousness remaining aware of reality, Spanos (1986) argues that the hidden observer is an artefact arising from the hypnotist's instructions.

Some practical applications of hypnotic phenomena

Whether hypnosis and hypnotic phenomena have any practical uses has also been the subject of much research. As has been seen, hypnosis can contribute to pain relief. Other applications are described below.

Hypermnesia and criminal investigations

Hypermnesia is the apparent ability of a hypnotised person to focus on selected details of an event and reconstruct an entire memory if told to do so. In some police departments, this has been used to prompt the memories of people who have witnessed a crime but cannot recall specific details of the events that occurred. Indeed, in America at least, evidence obtained from hypnotised witnesses has been admitted into court, and some police departments have officers trained in hypnosis.

In the *television technique*, the hypnotised witness is told that he or she will be able to 'zoom in' on details such as a car number plate and 'freeze the frame' to examine the details (Reiser & Nielsen, 1980). Unfortunately, the reports obtained from hypnotised people have not always been helpful. In an American court case (People versus Kempinski, 1980) a hypnotised witness identified Mr Kempinski as a victim's murderer. However, the defence successfully argued that, given the lighting conditions at the time, it would only have been possible to identify the murderer's face from a maximum of eight yards away. Since the witness was some 90 yards away, the defence challenged the validity of the witness' recall under hypnosis. The challenge was accepted and the evidence dismissed.

Box 4.8 *Some other cautions against the use of hypnosis in criminal investigations*

1 Witnesses may pick up on suggestions communicated by the hypnotist, incorporate these into memory, and recall them as 'factual'. Related to this is the finding that 'leading questions' are even more likely to produce distorted memories under hypnosis.
2 Although the hypnotically suggestible recall more information than non-hypnotised people, this information is frequently incorrect. Hypnotised witnesses sometimes report things that were not there and fail to report things that were.
3 The confidence with which hypnotised people give information is very high (even if it is actually incorrect). This may throw off both the police and a jury.
4 Hypnosis might not actually affect what people remember, but might make them less cautious about what they are willing to guess. If hypnosis does make mental images more vivid, hypnotised people may confuse these images with actual memories.

A panel appointed by the American Medical Association concluded that whilst hypnosis *sometimes* produces additional details, such information is often unreliable. Rather than accepting recall under hypnosis as evidence itself, the police were recommended to limit its use to the investigative stage of an enquiry, where it might produce new clues whose details could be checked by other sources of objective evidence.

Age regression

Hypnotised people seem to be able to play unusual roles. For example, something requiring increased stamina (such as riding a bicycle) can be done with apparently less fatigue than normal (Banyai & Hilgard, 1976). In *age regression*, people are asked to play themselves as infants or children. Some hypnotised people show excellent recall of childhood memories because hypnosis gives greater *access* to them, rather than effecting a literal return to an earlier stage of development (Oakley *et al.*, 1996).

Psychoanalytic theory

Hypnosis made a significant contribution to the development of *psychoanalytic theory*. Charcot, for example, believed that hysterical disorders (such as apparent blindness in the absence of any damage to the visual system) were caused by some sort of physical problem. However, his discovery that hysterical symptoms could be simulated under hypnosis led him to conclude that the origins of hysterical disorders were psychological rather than physical.

A little later, Breuer demonstrated that one of his patients could be made to feel better about her problems when she spoke freely of them under hypnosis. Freud believed that hypnosis was useful in gaining access to the unconscious and could be used to uncover the causes of mental disorders. For Freud, psychological problems in adulthood have their origins in early childhood experiences which cannot ordinarily be recalled because the memory of them has been *repressed* (Gross & McIlveen, 1998).

Box 4.9 *Regression*

Freud believed that hypnotic states produced *regression*. In this, the conscious control (or 'ego functioning') of behaviour is suspended, and it becomes possible to return to childish modes of behaviour. Although Freud later abandoned hypnosis as a method of gaining access to the unconscious (not least for the reason that he felt it elicited childhood *fantasies* rather than *experiences*), it is still used today to help people discuss memories whose apparent inaccessibility is hindering therapeutic progress (Hart & Hart, 1996). However, the approach has been criticised and the recent concerns about *false memory syndrome* have cast doubt on this particular application of hypnosis.

Hypnosis and behaviour control

According to some researchers, hypnotists are able to induce people to act in ways which grossly violate their moral code, and this is sometimes referred to as the *Hollywood theory of hypnosis* (Hayes, 1994). Such behaviours include harming others or doing damage to themselves. Other researchers, however, believe this to be untrue and also feel that it is impossible for a person to be tricked into behaving in such ways (Barber, 1969).

Reports of 'porno-hypnotist' shows in America, the use of 'striptease' in the stage show of at least one British hypnotist, and reports of indecent assaults on patients by hypnotherapists, have raised serious ethical questions about the extent to which hypnotists can control people's behaviour (Rogers, 1994). Because of this, it is hardly surprising that a Federation of Ethical Stage Hypnotists exists!

It is possible to think how a hypnotised person could be tricked into behaving in a way which violates ordinary standards of behaviour. For example, a situation could be misperceived by a hypnotised person who is told to shoot a gun at a 'paper target' which is actually another person (Carlson, 1987). What is much more difficult to determine is whether a particular behaviour occurs because the hypnotist has control or because the person actually wants to behave in that way.

Consider, for example, a person who is instructed to eat raw onions until told to stop. We might find that these instructions are followed and that the person feels angry and embarrassed by having been 'forced' to behave in such a way. Although it would appear that the hypnotist has been successful in producing a behaviour that would ordinarily not have been performed, we cannot rule out the possibility that the person *wanted* to be 'punished' in this way because of some real or imagined misdeed (Baron, 1989). As with all the other phenomena associated with hypnosis, there is still much for us to discover.

Conclusions

Hypnosis has attracted the interest of many researchers and hypnotic phenomena have been the subject of many experimental investigations. How hypnosis can best be explained is an issue yet to be resolved, although Alden (1995) has suggested that more and more researchers are moving towards accepting hypnosis as a 'non-state paradigm'. Whatever the explanation, hypnotic phenomena have been applied in several areas, although whether they contribute anything useful is far from clear.

Summary

- Serious scientific interest in hypnosis can be traced back to Mesmer and his belief that humans could be drawn together by **animal magnetism**. **Mesmerism**, a treatment for illnesses, supposedly rectified imbalances in the body's magnetic fields. It is likely, though, that any beneficial effects occurred through the **placebo effect**. Nevertheless, hypnosis has been used as an anaesthetic during surgery.

- There are several ways of inducing a hypnotic state and a number of characteristics associated with it. These include suspension of planning, accepting normally noticed inconsistencies, a narrowing of attention (resulting in less awareness of sensory information), and a responsiveness to suggestions to initiate and inhibit limb movements.

- Suggestibility also applies to perceptual distortions, including positive and negative hallucinations, post-hypnotic amnesia and post-hypnotic suggestion.

- There are individual differences in hypnotic susceptibility, and these can be measured using the **Stanford hypnotic susceptibility scale.** Hypnotic susceptibility is correlated with absorption, expectancy and fantasy-proneness, and there are neuropsychophysiological differences associated with hypnotic susceptibility.

- The genuineness of some hypnotic phenomena has been challenged. However, experimental studies of **trance logic** indicate that hypnotised people do behave differently from those merely pretending to be hypnotised. This, along with the finding that hypnotic susceptibility changes with age, points to hypnotic phenomena being genuine.

- **State (or special processes) theory** sees hypnosis as a unique and altered state of consciousness. Hilgard's **neo-dissociation theory** proposes that hypnosis is the dissociation (or division) of consciousness into separate channels of mental activity. This allows us to focus attention on the hypnotist and, simultaneously, to perceive other events peripherally (or sub-consciously).

- The **hidden observer phenomenon** and the **cold-pressor test** support Hilgard's theory. The analgesic properties of hypnosis can be explained by Hilgard's theory, although other explanations (relating to, for example, the production of endorphins) are equally plausible.

- The **non-state theory** sees hypnotised people as acting out social roles which are defined by their own expectations and the social situations in which they find themselves. It also involves the suspension of self-control. The theory is supported by the finding that susceptible hypnotic participants have vivid imaginations, and that behaviours possible under hypnosis are also possible in non-hypnotic conditions.

- The hidden observer phenomenon may simply be a product of a script supplied by the hypnotist. Rather than being a part of consciousness remaining aware of reality, non-state theorists view it as an artefact arising from the hypnotist's instructions.

- Hypnosis has been applied to criminal investigations, although the claims made by hypnotised people are often unreliable. As a result, evidence gathered under hypnosis must be treated with caution. **Age regression** has been used to recall long-forgotten childhood memories, probably because it gives greater access to them rather than literally returning a person to an earlier stage of development.

- Freud's **psychoanalytic theory** was influenced by the discovery that hysterical symptoms could be reproduced under hypnosis, and that some people felt better about their problems when speaking freely about them under hypnosis. Hypnosis is still used to help people recover repressed memories, but its use has been criticised because of its implication in **false memory syndrome**.

- The ethics of using hypnosis to induce behaviour change in public shows has been questioned. Whether it is possible for a hypnotist to cause people to behave in ways which grossly violate their moral code is a question yet to be answered.

SOME DRUGS AND THEIR EFFECTS ON BEHAVIOUR

5

Introduction and overview

For thousands of years, humans have taken drugs to alter their perceptions of reality and for thousands of years societies have limited this kind of drug use by placing various restrictions on it (Weil & Rosen, 1983). This chapter examines the psychological and physiological effects exerted by some *psychoactive drugs*. The word 'psychoactive' is usually taken to mean any chemical that alters perceptions and behaviour by changing conscious awareness. However, most drugs fit into this definition. Aspirin, for example, is psychoactive because when it relieves a headache, it changes conscious experience.

This chapter looks at drugs used to produce a temporarily altered state of consciousness for the purpose of *pleasure*. *Recreational drugs* have no legal restrictions and include alcohol, nicotine and caffeine. *Drugs of abuse* are also taken recreationally, but outside society's approval. These include cannabis, heroin, cocaine, amphetamine and ecstasy (Green, 1996a).

Tolerance, dependence, addiction and withdrawal

All of the drugs discussed in this chapter alter thoughts, feelings and behaviour by affecting the brain. However, the effects of some are *lessened* with continued use, and users need to take increasing amounts to achieve the same initial effect. This phenomenon is called *tolerance*.

Tolerance is sometimes associated with *physiological* (or *physical*) *dependence*. This means that the body cannot do without a drug because it has adjusted to, and becomes dependent on, that drug's presence. When the drug is stopped, various problems

occur, such as insomnia, profuse sweating, trembling, and hallucinations. These are symptoms of *withdrawal* (or *abstinence
syndrome*). Physical dependence and tolerance together define
the medical syndrome called *drug addiction*.

Some drugs are so pleasurable that users feel compelled to
continue taking them even though the body is not physically
dependent on the drug's presence. This is *psychological dependence*, and being deprived of the drug is anxiety-producing for
the user. Since the symptoms of anxiety (e.g. rapid pulse, profuse
sweating, and shaking) overlap with withdrawal symptoms, people may mistakenly believe they are physiologically dependent
on a drug.

Recreational drugs and drugs of abuse

Four major classes can be identified. *Depressants* (or *sedatives*)
depress neural activity, slow down bodily functions, induce
calmness and produce sleep. *Stimulants* temporarily excite neural
activity, arouse bodily functions, enhance positive feelings, and
heighten alertness. The *opiates* also depress activity in the central
nervous system, but have an *analgesic* property, and produce
pain insensitivity without loss of consciousness. *Hallucinogens*
produce alterations in perception and evoke sensory images in
the absence of any sensory input. As well as looking at the major
drugs in these four classes, we will also consider the effects of
cannabis, a drug which defies classification as one of the above.

The depressants

Depressants slow down mental processes and behaviours. The
most widely used and abused depressant is *alcohol*, whose effects
were known about 10,000 years ago (Hartston, 1996).

Alcohol

Over 90 per cent of adults in Britain drink alcohol to some
extent. There are wide individual differences in alcohol's effects,

which are at least in part dependent on body weight and gender. The effects of alcohol, and other drugs, also depend on *expectations*. People who believe alcohol has an arousing effect may be more responsive to sexual stimuli even though alcohol *per se* does not increase arousal.

In general, small amounts have a 'stimulating effect' (but alcohol is not a stimulant – see below). These include a lowering of social inhibitions, which interferes with the ability to foresee negative consequences and results in the inability to recall accepted standards of behaviour. Thus, actions may become more extreme and we are likely to 'speak our mind'. Large amounts have a sedative effect.

Box 5.1 *Alcohol and cognitive/motor functions*

Alcohol affects cognitive functions, such as processing recent experiences into long-term memory. A day after consuming a large amount of alcohol, a person might not remember the events that occurred when it was being taken. Other cognitive impairments include deficits in visual acuity and depth perception, and the subjective experience of time passing more quickly. Alcohol also affects motor functions. Even 10 mg interferes with the ability to follow a moving target with a pointer. 80 mg slows reaction time by about ten per cent. Greater amounts result in staggering and a complete loss of motor coordination caused by depression of neural activity in the cerebellum. Very large amounts can induce a coma or lead to death.

Although short-term use may alleviate depressive feelings, long-term use may augment such feelings. Heavy users suffer malnutrition because they eat less. Alcohol contains many calories, which suppresses appetite. Since alcohol interferes with the absorption of vitamin B from the intestines, it causes vitamin deficiency. The prolonged effect of this is brain damage, and memory is particularly affected. Other physical consequences include liver damage, heart disease, increased risk of a stroke, and susceptibility to infections due to a suppressed immune system. Women who drink during pregnancy can produce babies with *foetal alcohol syndrome*. This is characterised by retarded physical growth, intellectual development and motor coordination. There are also abnormalities in brain metabolic processes and liver functions.

After prolonged and severe intoxication, physiological dependence and withdrawal occur. The symptoms include restlessness, nausea, fever and the bizarre hallucinations of *delirium tremens*. In some cases, withdrawal produces such a profound shock to the body that death occurs. There is no doubt that tolerance develops, and it is likely that psychological dependence also develops.

Exactly how alcohol exerts its effects is not known. In terms of ANS activity, it has a relaxing effect. Its 'stimulating effects' probably occur from a suppression of the brain mechanisms that normally inhibit behaviour. In large amounts, alcohol decreases neural activity, possibly by acting on the cell membrane of neurons (especially those in the reticular activating system) and reducing their ability to conduct nerve impulses. Alcohol also seems to increase the sensitivity of post-synaptic receptors for the inhibitory neurotransmitter *gamma-amino butyric acid* (GABA). By increasing the inhibition generated by GABA, alcohol would reduce neural activity in the brain circuits associated with arousal.

Why some people abuse alcohol is also not clear. The *disease model of alcoholism* claims that some people have a weakness for it that cannot be controlled because of a genetic predisposition. If alcoholism is to be cured, the alcoholic must abstain *completely* (the philosophy of *Alcoholics Anonymous*). Alternatively, drinking may be a complex category of behaviour with different causes and hence different cures. According to the *social model of alcoholism*, excessive alcohol consumption can be treated by *controlled drinking* rather than abstinence. This approach implies that people can be taught to maintain consumption at an acceptable (non-damaging) level.

Barbiturates, tranquillisers and solvents

Barbiturates are also depressants and have similar effects to alcohol. Because they depress neural activity, they are often prescribed to induce sleep or reduce anxiety. They exert their effects by reducing the release of excitatory neurotransmitters at synapses in several parts of the nervous system. Barbiturates were first used clinically in 1903. However, their clinical use is limited because of physiological dependence, withdrawal and tolerance. Other depressants include 'minor tranquillisers' (such as *Valium*) and *aromatic solvents*. 'Minor tranquillisers' have much milder effects than barbiturates and do not induce sleep. Aromatic solvents include some types of glue and paint thinner. Their use in Britain has been associated with a number of deaths and various surveys have estimated that about six to nine per cent of secondary school children (around 500,000) have abused solvents (Mihill, 1997).

The stimulants

The general effects of stimulants is to stimulate the CNS by increasing the transmission of nerve impulses. The most widely consumed legal stimulants are *caffeine* and *nicotine*, both of which exert mild effects. *Amphetamines* and *cocaine* exert considerably stronger effects and are illegal, as are the newer 'designer' stimulants such as *methylenedioxymethamphetamine* (or *MDMA*) which is known as '*ecstasy*'. 'Designer' drugs are synthetic substances produced by altering the chemical structure of illegal substances without reducing their potency.

Amphetamines

The amphetamines were first synthesised in the 1920s. Their general effect is to increase energy and enhance self-confidence. As a result, they were used extensively by the military in World War Two to reduce fatigue and give soldiers going into battle more confidence. Another effect is to suppress appetite, and they also found use as 'slimming pills' being marketed under such trade names as Methedrine, Dexedrine and Benzedrine. However, their effects on consciousness and behaviour led to them being widely abused.

Box 5.2 *Some uses of amphetamines*

Chemically, amphetamines are similar to *adrenaline*. This has led to amphetamines being used as a treatment for asthma, since they open respiratory passages and ease breathing. Amphetamines are also used in the treatment of *narcolepsy*, a disorder characterised by brief and unpredictable periods of sleep.

One other use of amphetamines is in the treatment of attention-deficit/hyperactivity disorder (ADHD) in children. With these children, amphetamines and a related stimulant, methylphenidate hydrochloride (*Ritalin*) increase self-control and attention span and decrease fidgeting.

Amphetamines are swallowed in pill form, inhaled through the nose in powder form, or injected in liquid form. Small amounts cause increased wakefulness, alertness and arousal. Users experience a sense of energy and confidence, and feel that any problem can be solved and any task accomplished. This effect is, however, illusory, and problem-solving is no easier with the drug than without it. After the drug wears off, users experience a 'crash' (characterised by extreme fatigue and depression). They counteract this by taking the drug again which can have serious long-term consequences (see below). Large amounts cause restlessness, hallucinations and *paranoid delusions*.

Amphetamines can stimulate aggressive, violent behaviour. This is not due *directly* to the drug itself. Rather, the effect occurs as a result of personality changes that come from excessive use. The paranoid delusions experienced in *amphetamine psychosis* are virtually indistinguishable from those experienced in *paranoid schizophrenia*. Long-term use has also been associated with severe depression, suicidal tendencies, disrupted thinking and brain damage.

Tolerance develops quickly as does psychological dependence. The evidence concerning physiological dependence is mixed. However, the amphetamine 'hangover' (characterised by extreme fatigue, depression, prolonged sleep, irritability, disorientation and agitated motor activity) is indicative of a withdrawal effect, suggesting that a physiological dependence has developed (Blum, 1984).

Cocaine

Cocaine, or more properly cocaine hydrochloride, is a powerful central nervous system (CNS) stimulant extracted from the leaves of the coca shrub which is native to the Andes Mountains in South America. It was discovered centuries ago by Peruvian Indians who chewed on the plant leaves to increase stamina and relieve fatigue and hunger. Among present-day South Americans, leaf chewing is still practised.

Box 5.3 *Cocaine, Coca-Cola and Freud*

Cocaine became known in Europe in the middle 1800s, when coca was blended into wine and other drinks. Until 1906, Coca-Cola actually *did* contain cocaine. Today, it is still blended with coca leaves that have had their active ingredient removed! Sigmund Freud used cocaine to fight his own depression and supported its use as, amongst other things, a cure for alcoholism. He eventually became disillusioned with the drug because of its side-effects. One of his friends, however, developed its use as a local anaesthetic: in very high concentrations cocaine blocks the transmission of action potentials in axons. Today, this is still the drug's only legitimate use.

Cocaine is inhaled through the nose in powder form, injected into the veins in liquid form, or smoked. When smoked, the drug reaches the brain in 5–10 seconds, as compared with 30–120 seconds when inhaled and 60–180 seconds when injected (Miller *et al.*, 1989). It can also be swallowed, rubbed on the gums, or blown into the throat.

In general, cocaine's effects are similar to amphetamine, though of a briefer duration (around 15–30 minutes as compared with several hours). This is because cocaine is metabolised much more quickly. Typically, the user experiences a state of euphoria, deadening of pain, increased self-confidence and energy, and enhanced attention. As with amphetamines, users experience a 'crash' when the drug wears off. Attempts to offset these effects include taking depressants or opiates.

Even in small amounts, the stimulating effects can result in cardiac arrest and death. Repeated inhalation constricts the blood vessels in the nose. The nasal septum may become perforated, necessitating cosmetic surgery. *Cocaine psychosis* (cf. amphetamine psychosis) can also occur with chronic long-term use as can convulsions, respiratory failure and bleeding into the brain. At least in rats, cocaine gradually lowers the tolerance for seizures (Bales, 1986). An interesting effect is *formication*, the sensation that 'insects' ('coke bugs') are crawling beneath the skin. Although this is merely random neural activity, users sometimes try to remove the imaginary insects by cutting deep into themselves with a knife. Cocaine taken in pregnancy has been associated with impaired foetal development.

Whether cocaine produces physiological dependence, tolerance and withdrawal has been the subject of much debate. However, there is no argument that it produces psychological dependence. This probably stems from the user's desire to avoid the severe depression associated with 'crashing' (and some researchers see the symptoms associated with 'crashing' as indicative of physiological dependence: Miller *et al.*, 1989).

Both amphetamine and cocaine stimulate the sympathetic nervous system causing the effects observed with increased ANS activity. The increase in brain activation may be due to heightened activity at synapses that secrete noradrenaline and dopamine. Amphetamine and cocaine facilitate the release of noradrenaline and dopamine, but inhibit their re-uptake by the vesicles that released them. This results in an excess of these neurotransmitters, which increases neuronal activity and leads to a persistent state of arousal.

The euphoric effects are probably the result of the drug's effects on dopamine, whilst the increased energy is probably caused by noradrenaline. According to Carlson (1987), cocaine activates neural circuits that are normally triggered by reinforcing events such as eating or sexual contact. Cocaine can thus be seen as an artificial producer of some of the effects of these activities. The 'crash' associated with cocaine and amphetamine use is held to be a result of the 'rush' depleting the brain of noradrenaline and dopamine.

Box 5.4 *Crack*

Crack is a form of cocaine which first appeared in the 1980s. It is made using cocaine hydrochloride, ammonia or baking soda, and water. When heated, the baking soda produces a 'cracking' sound. The result is a crystal which has had the hydrochloride base removed (hence the term *free basing* to describe its production). Its effects are more rapid and intense than cocaine. However, the 'crash' is also more intense, and the pleasurable effects wear off more rapidly.

MDMA

MDMA or 'ecstasy' is a chemical relative of amphetamine, first synthesised in 1912, and later patented as an appetite suppressant, though never marketed. It is swallowed in pill or tablet form, and sometimes taken with other mood-altering drugs. Small amounts produce a mild euphoric 'rush', together with feelings of elation. This can last for ten hours. Self-confidence is increased and sexual confidence gained. Large amounts trigger hallucinations. Users report MDMA's effects to be intermediate between amphetamine and LSD (see page 85). Serotonin and dopamine are the neurotransmitters affected.

Ecstasy causes extreme dehydration and hyperthermia which leads to a form of heatstroke. This can produce convulsions, collapse and death. Blood pressure also rises dangerously. If it becomes too high the taker may suffer a stroke and thereafter permanent brain damage. Over 50 deaths in Britain alone have been attributed to the drug (Parrott, 1997). The high temperature dance environment of Britain's 'rave' scene no doubt increases the hyperthermia. Depression and panic attacks are also associated with long-term use, as are kidney and liver failure (Green, 1996b).

As Parrott & Yeomans (1995) have observed, little research has been carried out into the effects of ecstasy, let alone the effects of abstinence, despite the fact that several million doses of the drug are annually consumed worldwide. According to the Department of Health (1994), tolerance occurs but physiological dependence does not.

The opiates

The psychological effects of the sticky resin produced by the unripe seed pods of the opium poppy have been known for centuries. The ancient Sumerians, in 4000 BC, gave the poppy its name: it means 'plant of joy'. One constituent of opium is *morphine*. From morphine, two other opiates can be extracted. These are *codeine* and *heroin*.

Morphine and heroin

In general, the opiates depress neural functioning and suppress physical sensations and responses to stimulation. For reasons which will become clear shortly, the opiates are effective in reducing pain. In Europe, morphine was first used as an analgesic during the Franco-Prussian war. However, it quickly became apparent that it produced physiological dependence, which became known as 'the soldier's disease'. In 1898, in an attempt to cure this physiological dependence, the Bayer Company of Germany developed heroin (so named because it was the 'hero' that would cure the 'soldier's disease'). Unfortunately, heroin also causes physiological dependence and has many unpleasant side-effects.

Heroin can be smoked, inhaled through the nostrils, or intravenously injected. Users call the immediate effects the 'rush', which is described as an overwhelming sensation of pleasure similar to sexual orgasm but affecting the whole body. Subjectively, such effects are so pleasurable that they eradicate any thoughts of food or sex. Heroin rapidly decomposes into morphine which produces feelings of euphoria, well-being, relaxation and drowsiness.

In long-term users, increases in aggressiveness and social isolation have been reported as has a decrease in general physical activity. Although the findings relating to physical damage are mixed, the use of any opiate may damage the body's immune system leading to increased susceptibility to infection. The impurity of heroin sold to users, their lack of an adequate diet, and the risks from contaminated needles, also increase the dangers to health. Overdoses are common, but drugs like *naloxone* act as opiate antagonists (it blocks the pain-relieving effects of morphine), although their effects are not long-lasting and they cannot control heroin use.

Heroin use produces both physiological and psychological dependence. Tolerance develops very quickly. Withdrawal symptoms initially involve the experience of flu-like symptoms. These progress to tremors, stomach cramps and chills, which alternate with sweating, rapid pulse, high blood pressure, insomnia and diarrhoea. Often, the skin breaks out into goose bumps resembling a plucked turkey (hence the term 'cold turkey' to describe attempts to abstain). The legs also jerk uncontrollably (hence the term 'kicking the habit'). Such symptoms usually disappear within one week.

Box 5.5   *Heroin and endorphins*

The brain produces its own opiates (*opioid peptides* or *endorphins*). When we engage in behaviours important to our survival, endorphins are released into the fluid that bathes brain cells. Endorphin molecules stimulate *opiate receptors* on some brain neurons. These are similar to those post-synaptic receptors that respond to neurotransmitters. One consequence of this is an intensely pleasurable effect just like that reported by heroin users. This has led some researchers to suggest that endorphins are important in mood regulation. Another consequence is analgesia.

According to Snyder (1977), regularly taking opiates overloads endorphin sites in the brain, and the brain stops its own production of them. When the user abstains, neither the naturally occurring endorphins nor the opiates are available. The internal mechanism for regulating pain is thus severely disrupted and the person experiences the painful withdrawal symptoms described earlier.

Methadone

To treat the physiological dependence associated with opiate use, several synthetic opiates (or opioids) have been created. One of these is *methadone*, which acts more slowly than heroin and does not produce the 'rush' associated with heroin use. Whether methadone is a suitable substitute is debatable. Whilst methadone users are less likely to take heroin, they are still taking a drug and likely to become at least psychologically dependent on it, so that the withdrawal symptoms associated with heroin can be avoided.

The hallucinogens

Hallucinogens produce the most profound effects on consciousness. For that reason they are sometimes called *psychedelics* (which means 'mind expanding' or 'mind manifesting'). Their effects include changes in perception, thought processes and emotions. Two of the most well-researched hallucinogens are naturally derived. *Mescaline* comes from the peyote cactus, whilst *psilocybin* is obtained from the mushroom *Psilocybe mexicana* (the so-called 'magic mushroom'). Others, such as *lysergic acid diethylamide* (LSD) and *phencyclidine* (PCP), are chemically synthesised.

LSD

LSD was first synthesised in 1943 by Hoffmann, a Swiss chemist. After accidentally ingesting some of the chemical, Hoffmann reported that he:

'perceived an uninterrupted stream of fantastic pictures, extraordinary shapes with intense, kaleidoscopic play of colours'.

In the 1960s, LSD was used for a variety of purposes including the treatment of emotional and behavioural disturbances, and as a pain reliever for the terminally ill. It was also believed that LSD could serve useful military purposes (Neill, 1987). Its popularity as a 'recreational' drug was largely inspired by Timothy Leary, a Harvard University psychologist, who coined the slogan 'turn on, tune in, and drop out', used by the 1960s' hippy movement.

LSD is usually impregnated on blotting paper and swallowed. Unlike other drugs, the onset of its effects may be delayed for an hour or more. LSD produces heightened and distorted sensory experiences, such as sights and sounds being intensified or changing form and colour. Hallucinations may also be tactile. Such effects may be pleasurable or terrifying (a 'bad trip') depending on mood and expectations. The subjective passage of time is distorted and appears to slow dramatically. *Synaesthesia*, the blending of sensory experiences, may also occur. Music, for example, may yield visual sensations. *Depersonalisation* has also been reported and is experienced as a state in which the body is perceived as being separate from the self. Users report being able to see themselves from afar. Impaired judgement also occurs, even though the subjective feeling may be of an 'increased understanding' of the world.

Some long-term users experience *flashbacks*, distorted perceptions or hallucinations occurring days or weeks after the drug was taken. These might be physiological or psychological in origin. There is no evidence to suggest that LSD itself can cause death, but there are numerous examples of users being killed as a result of its psychological effects. Reproductive processes also seem to be affected by long-term use, since women are less likely to conceive when they are taking the drug. The reason for this is not known.

LSD use does not seem to lead to physiological dependence and withdrawal. However, tolerance can develop rapidly. If taken repeatedly, few effects are produced until its administration is stopped for about a week. Whether LSD produces psychological dependence is hotly debated (McWilliams & Tuttle, 1973).

The chemical structure of some hallucinogens closely resembles dopamine and serotonin. According to Jacobs (1987), hallucinogen molecules compete with the normal activity of these neurotransmitters in the brain. Serotonin may play a role in the production of dream-like activity (see Chapter 2). The inhibition of neural circuits responsible for dreaming at any time other than during sleep might explain why we do not dream during the waking hours. However, suppression of serotonin by hallucinogenic drug molecules might cause 'dream mechanisms' to be activated, with the result that the person experiences a 'waking dream' or hallucination (Carlson, 1988).

Box 5.6   *The form of hallucinations*

Siegel (1982) has suggested that all hallucinations, whether caused by drugs, oxygen starvation or sensory deprivation, take the same form. Usually they begin with simple geometric forms (such as a spiral), continue with more meaningful images (such as 'replays' of past emotional experiences) and, at the peak of the hallucination, produce a feeling of separation from the body and dream-like experiences which can appear frighteningly real. The fact that all hallucinations seem to take the same form suggests that the same mechanisms may be involved in their production.

Phencyclidine (PCP)

PCP ('angel dust') was first synthesised in the 1950s for use as a surgical anaesthetic. However, this was discontinued when its psychoactive side-effects became apparent. Usually combined with tobacco and smoked, it can be classified as a hallucinogen because it produces distortions in body image and depersonalisation. In small amounts, users report euphoria, heightened awareness, and a sense that all problems have disappeared. With large amounts, however, it has stimulant, depressant, and (not surprisingly given its original purpose) analgesic properties. Effects include violence, panic, psychotic behaviour, disrupted motor activity and chronic depression. These may persist for weeks after the drug has been taken.

Long-term use of PCP is associated with what Smith *et al.* (1978) call the four 'Cs': *combativeness* (agitated or violent behaviour), *catatonia* (muscular rigidity of the body), *convulsions* (epileptic-like seizures) and *coma* (a deep, unresponsive sleep). Users also report difficulty in thinking clearly and emotional blandness. Although PCP does not produce physiological dependence, users may become psychologically dependent (Bolter *et al.*, 1976).

Cannabis

Cannabis is one of the most widely used drugs, second only in popularity to alcohol. The *cannabis sativa* plant grows wild in many parts of the world and was cultivated over 5000 years ago in China. The plant's psychoactive ingredient is *delta-9-tetrahydrocannabinol* or THC. THC is found in the branches and leaves of the male and female plants (*marijuana*), but is highly concentrated in the resin of the female plant. *Hashish* (or 'hash') is derived from the sticky resin and is more potent than marijuana.

Cannabis is usually smoked with tobacco or is eaten. When smoked, THC finds its way to the brain inside seven seconds. Small amounts produce a mild, pleasurable 'high', consisting of relaxation, a loss of social inhibition, intoxication, and a humorous mood. Speech becomes slurred and coordination is impaired. Other effects include increased heart rate, lack of concentration and enhanced appetite. Short-term memory is also affected, and there is an inability to retain information for later use. It is not unusual for a user to begin a sentence and then forget what the sentence was about before it has been completed. As with other drugs, the effects are influenced by social context and other factors. Thus, some users report negative effects such as fear, anxiety and confusion.

Large amounts result in hallucinogenic reactions, including the perceived slowing of time and amplified sensitivity to colours, sounds, tastes and smells. However, these subjective reports are not borne out by objective measures. As well as increased awareness of bodily states (such as heart rate), sexual sensations are also heightened.

THC remains in the body for as long as a month. Cannabis may disrupt the male sex hormones and, in females, influence the menstrual cycle. Its use during pregnancy has been associated with impaired foetal growth, and cannabis is more damaging to the throat and lungs than cigarette smoking. Long-term use may lead to *amotivational syndrome* (a general lack of energy or motivation). However, this may simply reflect the fact that users differ psychologically from non-users.

There is some debate over whether cannabis leads to physiological dependence. Tolerance is a sign of physiological dependence, but with cannabis *reverse tolerance* has been reported. Thus, regular use leads to a *lowering* of the amount needed to achieve the initial effects. This could be due to a build-up of THC which takes a long time to be metabolised. An alternative explanation is that users become more adept at inhaling the drug and therefore perceive its effects more quickly. Withdrawal effects (restlessness, irritability and insomnia) have been reported, but these seem to be associated with the continuous use of very large amounts. Psychological dependence almost certainly occurs in at least some people.

> **Box 5.7** *Some medical uses of cannabis*
>
> Cannabis has some *medical* applications. For example, it has been used with glaucoma sufferers because it reduces fluid pressure in the eyes. The fact that cannabis decreases nausea and vomiting has also led to a tablet form (*Nabilane*) being administered to patients with cancer who must receive chemotherapy, a treatment that induces nausea and vomiting. A third medical application is with multiple sclerosis. Smoking cannabis reduces muscle spasm, tremors, night leg pain and depression (Dillner, 1997).

Cannabis has been classified as a hallucinogen because large amounts produce hallucinations. However, it could also be classified as a stimulant because it also has a stimulant effect. In very large amounts, however, it acts as a depressant.

The precise biochemical mechanisms underlying THC's behavioural effects are not known. It may influence the action of noradrenaline and serotonin. Acetylcholine plays a role in memory, and the observation that cannabis interferes with the ability to recall previously learned information might be explained in terms of the disruption of normal activity in acetylcholine-utilising neurons in the limbic system.

Conclusions

This chapter has examined the physiological and psychological effects of some of the legal and illegal drugs taken for the purpose of pleasure. The effects produced by the drugs are wide-ranging, as are their effects on brain chemistry.

Summary

- **Psychoactive drugs** are chemicals which alter perceptions and behaviour by changing conscious awareness. **Recreational drugs** (e.g. alcohol) have no legal restrictions. **Drugs of abuse** (e.g. cannabis) are also taken recreationally, but are outside society's approval.

- **Physiological (or physical) dependence** is the body's inability to do without a drug. When the drug is stopped, the symptoms of **withdrawal** occur. **Tolerance** is the need for more of a drug to achieve its initial effects. Physical dependence coupled with tolerance defines **drug addiction**. A drug that compels people to take it, even though there is no physical dependence, produces **psychological dependence**.

- **Depressants** (e.g. alcohol, barbiturates, minor tranquillisers and aromatic solvents) slow down mental processes and behaviour. Small amounts of alcohol suppress brain mechanisms that normally inhibit behaviour. Large amounts relax ANS activity and decrease neural activity, possibly by acting on the cell membranes of neurons and reducing their ability to conduct nerve impulses. Alcohol also reduces neural activity by increasing the sensitivity of post-synaptic receptors for GABA, an inhibitory neurotransmitter.

- **Stimulants** (e.g. caffeine, nicotine, amphetamine, MDMA and cocaine) stimulate CNS activity by increasing the transmission of nerve impulses. The powerful stimulants increase energy and self-confidence, and produce euphoria and elation.

- The long-term consequences associated with amphetamine and cocaine include the development of symptoms indistinguishable from paranoid schizophrenia. These stimulants facilitate the release of noradrenaline (associated with increased energy) and dopamine (associated with euphoria), but inhibit their re-uptake by the vesicles that released them.

- **MDMA** is a chemical relative of amphetamine. Small amounts produce mild euphoria and increased self- and sexual confidence. Large amounts trigger hallucinations. Long-term consequences include extreme dehydration and hyperthermia, which can result in convulsions and death.

- The **opiates** include codeine, morphine, heroin and methadone. Their general effect is to depress neural functioning and suppress physical sensations and responses to pain. Regular taking of heroin overloads the brain's opiate receptors and the brain stops producing endorphins. When the user abstains, the absence of endorphins produces painful withdrawal symptoms.

- Some **hallucinogens** (e.g. mescaline and psilocybin) are naturally occurring. Others (e.g. LSD and PCP) are chemically synthesised. Hallucinogens cause changes in perception, thought processes and emotions. Hallucinations may be a result of serotonin's suppression by hallucinogenic drug molecules. Synaesthesia and depersonalisation are also associated with LSD use. Long-term consequences include flashbacks and tolerance, although LSD use is not associated with physiological dependence and withdrawal.

- PCP causes distortions in body image and depersonalisation and, in small amounts, euphoria and heightened awareness. Large amounts have stimulant, depressant and analgesic properties. Behavioural effects include violence, panic, psychotic behaviour, disrupted motor activity and chronic depression. Long-term use is associated with combatitiveness, catatonia, convulsions and coma, as well as psychological dependence.

- Small amounts of **cannabis** produce relaxation, loss of social inhibition and a humorous mood. However, short-term memory is impaired, concentration is reduced and appetite increased. Large amounts produce a perceived slowing down of time, heightened sensory sensitivity, and an increased awareness of bodily states. Sexual sensations are also increased.

- THC, the psychoactive chemical in cannabis, can disrupt hormonal activity in both sexes. Used during pregnancy, cannabis can impair foetal growth. Long-term use may produce **amotivational syndrome**, and is associated with **reverse tolerance**. Cannabis may exert its effects by influencing noradrenaline, serotonin and acetylcholine.

REFERENCES

ADAM, K. & OSWALD, I. (1977) Sleep is for tissue restoration. *Journal of the Royal College of Physicians*, 11, 376–388.

ADAM, K. & OSWALD, I. (1983) Protein synthesis, bodily renewal and the sleep-wake cycle. *Clinical Science*, 65, 561–567.

ADAM, M.N. (1983) 'Time of Day Effects in Memory for Text.' (D.Phil. thesis, University of Sussex.)

ALDEN, P. (1995) Hypnosis – the professional's perspective. *The Psychologist*, 8, 78.

ASCHOFF, J. & WEVER, R. (1981) The circadian system in man. In J. Aschoff (Ed.) *Handbook of Behavioural Neurology* (Volume 4). New York: Plenum Press.

ASERINSKY, E. & KLEITMAN, N. (1953) Regularly occurring periods of eye motility and concomitant phenomena during sleep. *Science*, 118, 273–274.

BALES, J. (1986) New studies cite drug use dangers. *APA Monitor*, 17 (11), 26.

BANYAI, E.I. & HILGARD, E.R. (1976) A comparison of active-alert hypnotic induction with traditional relaxation induction. *Journal of Abnormal Psychology*, 85, 218–224.

BARBER, T.X. (1969) *Hypnosis: A Scientific Approach*. New York: Von Nostrand.

BARBER, T.X. (1970) *LSD, Marijuana, Yoga And Hypnosis*. Chicago: Aldine Press.

BARBER, T.X. (1979) Suggested ('hypnotic') behaviour: The trance paradigm versus an alternative paradigm. In E. Fromm & R.E. Shor (Eds) *Hypnosis: Developments in Research and New Perspectives*. Chicago: Aldine Press.

BARON, R.A. (1989) *Psychology: The Essential Science*. London: Allyn & Bacon.

BATES, B.L. (1993) Individual differences in response to hypnosis. In J.W. Rhue, S.J. Lynn & I. Kirsch (Eds) *Handbook of Clinical Hypnosis*. Washington, D.C.: American Psychological Association.

BERRY, D.T.R. & WEBB, W.B. (1983) State measures and sleep stages. *Psychological Reports*, 52, 807–812.

BIANCHI, A. (1992) Dream chemistry. *Harvard Magazine*, September–October, 21–22.

BLAKE, M.J.F. (1971) Temperament and time of day. In W.P. Colquhoun (Ed.) *Biological Rhythms and Human Performance*. London: Academic Press.

BLOCH, V. (1976) Brain activation and memory consolidation. In Rosenzweig, M.A. & Bennett, E.L. (Eds) *Neural Mechanisms of Learning and Memory*. Cambridge, MA: MIT Press.

BLUM, K. (1984) *Handbook of Abusable Drugs*. New York: Gardner Press.

BOKERT, E. (1970) The effects of thirst and related auditory stimulation on dream reports. Paper presented to the Association for the Physiological Study of Sleep, Washington DC.

BOLTER, A., HEMINGER, A., MARTIN, G. & FRY, M. (1976) Outpatient clinical experience in a community drug abuse program with phencyclidine. *Clinical Toxicology*, 9, 593–600.

BORBELY, A. (1986) *Secrets of Sleep*. Harmondsworth: Penguin.

BOWERS, K.S. (1976) *Hypnosis for the Seriously Curious*. Monterey, CA: Brooks Cole.

BROWN, J. (1996) Playing for time. *The Sunday Times Style Magazine*, 27 October, 36.

CARLSON, N.R. (1987) *Discovering Psychology*. London: Allyn & Bacon.

CARLSON, N.R. (1988) *Foundations of Physiological Psychology*. Boston: Allyn & Bacon.

CARTWRIGHT, R.D. (1978) *A Primer on Sleep and Dreaming*. Reading, MA: Addison-Wesley.

CHASE, M. & MORALES, F. (1990) The atonia and myoclonia of active (REM) sleep. *Annual Review of Psychology*, 41, 557–584.

COE, W.C. & YASHINSKI, E. (1985) Volitional experiences associated with breaching post-hypnotic amnesia. *Journal of Personality and Social Psychology*, 48, 716–722.

COHEN, D.B. (1973) Sex role orientation and dream recall. *Journal of Abnormal Psychology*, 82, 246–252.

COLLEE, J. (1993) Symbol minds. *The Observer Life Magazine*, 26 September, 14.

COREN, S. (1996) *Sleep Thieves*. New York: Free Press.

COUNCIL, J.R., KIRSCH, I. & HAFNER, L.P. (1986) Expectancy versus absorption in the prediction of hypnotic responding. *Journal of Personality and Social Psychology*, 50, 182–189.

CRAWFORD, H.J. (1994) Brain dynamics and hypnosis: Attentional and disattentional processes. *International Journal of Clinical and Experimental Hypnosis*, 42, 204–231.

CRICK, F. & MITCHISON, G. (1983) The function of dream sleep. *Nature*, 304, 111–114.

DALTON, K. (1964) *The Premenstrual Syndrome*. Springfield, ILL: Charles C. Thomas.

DEMENT, W.C. (1960) The effects of dream deprivation. *Science*, 131, 1705–1707.

DEMENT, W.C. (1974) *Some Must Watch While Some Must Sleep*. San Francisco: W.H. Freeman.

DEMENT, W.C. & KLEITMAN, N. (1957) Cyclical variations in EEG during sleep and their relation to eye movements, body motility and dreaming. *Electroencephalography and Clinical Neurophysiology*, 9, 673–690.

DEMENT, W.C. & WOLPERT, E. (1958) The relation of eye movements, body motility and external stimuli to dream content. *Journal of Experimental Psychology*, 55, 543–553.

DEPARTMENT OF HEALTH (1994) *Drugs: A Parent's Guide*. Central Print Unit.

DILLNER, L. (1997) Joint action. *The Guardian*, 15 April, 9.

EMPSON, J.A.C. (1989) *Sleep and Dreaming*. London: Faber and Faber.

EMPSON, J.A.C. & CLARKE, P.R.F. (1970) Rapid eye movements and remembering. *Nature*, 228, 287–288.

EVANS, C. (1984) *Landscapes of the Night: How and Why We Dream*. New York: Viking.

FISHER, S. & GREENBERG, R. (1977) *Scientific Credibility of Freud's Theories*. New York: Basic Books.

FOULKES, D. (1971) Longitudinal studies of dreams in children. In Masserman, J. (Ed.) *Science and Psychoanalysis*. New York: Grune & Stratton.

FOULKES, D. (1985) *Dreaming: A Cognitive-Psychological Analysis*. Hillsdale, NJ: Lawrence Erlbaum Associates.

FREUD, S. (1900) *The Interpretation of Dreams*. London: Hogarth Press.

GREEN, S. (1996a) Drugs and behaviour. *Psychology Review*, 3, 14–17.

GREEN, S. (1996b) Ecstasy. *Psychology Review*, 3, 34.

GREENBERG, R. & PEARLMAN, C. (1967) Delerium tremens and dreaming. *American Journal of Psychiatry*, 124, 133–142.

GREENBERG, R., PILLARD, R. & PEARLMAN, C. (1972) The effect of dream (stage REM) deprivation on adaptation to stress. *Psychosomatic Medicine*, 34, 257–262.

GROSS, R. & McILVEEN, R. (1998) *Psychology: A New Introduction*. London: Hodder & Stoughton.

HALL, C. & VAN DE CASTLE, R.L. (1966) *The Content Analysis of Dreams*. E. Norwalk, CT: Appleton-Century-Crofts.

HALL, C.S. (1966) *The Meaning of Dreams*. New York: McGraw-Hill.

HARDIE, E.A. (1997) PMS in the workplace: Dispelling the myth of the cyclic dysfunction. *Journal of Occupational and Organisational Psychology*, 70, 97–102.

HART, B.B., & ALDEN, P. (1994) Hypnotic techniques in the control of pain. In H.B. Gibson (Ed.) *Psychology, Pain and Anaesthesia*. London: Chapman & Hall.

HART, C. & HART, B.B. (1996) The use of hypnosis with children and adolescents. *The Psychologist*, 9, 506–509.

HARTMANN, E.L. (1973) *The Functions of Sleep*. New Haven, CT: Yale University Press.

HARTSTON, W. (1996) A history of the world in 10½ inches: 21 – Alcohol. *The Independent (Section 2)*, 19 September, 30.

HAYES, N. (1994) *Foundations of Psychology: An Introductory Text*. London: Routledge.

HEAP, B. (1996) The nature of hypnosis. *The Psychologist*, 9, 498–501.

HERMAN, J. & ROFFWARG, H. (1983) Modifying oculomotor activity in awake subjects increases the amplitude of eye movement during REM sleep. *Science*, 220, 1074–1076.

HIGHFIELD, R. (1996a) Scientists shed light on the origins of our body clock. *The Daily Telegraph*, 5 May, 6.

HIGHFIELD, R. (1996b) Working out how time flies. *The Daily Telegraph*, 21 February, 14.

HIGHFIELD, R. (1996c) While you were dreaming … *The Daily Telegraph*, 2 October, 14.

HILGARD, E.R. (1973) A neodissociation interpretation of pain reduction in hypnosis. *Psychological Review*, 80, 396–411.

HILGARD, E.R. (1977) *Divided Consciousness: Multiple Controls in Human Thought and Action*. New York: Wiley-Interscience.

HOBSON, J.A. (1988) *The Dreaming Brain*. New York: Basic Books.

HOBSON, J.A. (1989) Dream theory: A new view of the brain-mind. *The Harvard Medical School Mental Health Letter*, 5, 3–5.

HOBSON, J.A. & McCARLEY, R.W. (1977) The brain as a dream state generator: An activation-synthesis hypothesis of the dream process. *American Journal of Psychiatry*, 134, 1335–1348.

HOLLINGTON, S. (1995) Sweet dreams are made of this. *The Observer*, 12 March, 3.

HORNE, J.A. & OSTERBERG, O. (1976) A self-assessment questionnaire to determine morningness-eveningness in human circadian rhythms. *International Journal of Chronobiology*, 4, 97–190.

HÜBER-WEIDMAN, H. (1976) *Sleep, Sleep Disturbances and Sleep Deprivation*. Cologne: Kiepenheuser & Witsch.

HUGGETT, C. & ALDCROFT, C. (1996) The experience of living in a secluded cave for a month. *Proceedings of the British Psychological Society 27th Annual Student Conference, School of Education, University of Wales*, Cardiff, 27 April.

IRWIN, A. (1996) Five days go missing as student plays her bagpipes. *The Daily Telegraph*, 28 September, 1.

IRWIN, A. (1997) People 'not designed for night work'. *The Daily Telegraph*, 22 September, 6.

JACOBS, B.L. (1987) How hallucinogenic drugs work. *American Scientist*, 75, 386–392.

JOUVET, M. (1967) Mechanisms of the states of sleep: A neuropharmacological approach. *Research Publications of the Association for the Research in Nervous and Mental Diseases*, 45, 86–126.

JOUVET, M. (1983) Hypnogenic indolamine-dependent factors and paradoxical sleep rebound. In Monnier, E. & Meulders, A. (Eds) *Functions of the Nervous System*, Volume 4: *Psychoneurobiology*. New York: Elsevier.

KALES, A., KALES, J.D. & BIXLER, E.O. (1974) Insomnia: An approach to management and treatment. *Psychiatric Annals*, 4, 28–44.

KINNUNEN, T., ZAMANSKY, H.S. & BLOCK, M.L. (1995) Is the hypnotised subject lying? *Journal of Abnormal Psychology*, 103, 184–191.

KIRSCH, I. & COUNCIL, J.R. (1992) Situational and personality correlates of hypnotic responsiveness. In E. Fromm & M.R. Nash (Eds) *Contemporary Hypnosis Research*. New York: Guildford Press.

KLEITMAN, N. (1963) *Sleep and Wakefulness* (2nd edition). Chicago: University of Chicago Press.

KOUKKOU, M. & LEHMAN, D. (1980) Psychophysiologie des Traumens und der Neurosentherapie: Das Zustands-Wechsel Modell, eine Synopsis. Fortschritte der Neurologie, *Psychiatrie unter ihrer Grenzgebeite*, 48, 324–350.

LE FANU, J. (1994) May I examine your dream? *The Times*, 13 January, 15.

LOOMIS, A.L., HARVEY, E.N. & HOBART, A. (1937) Cerebral states during sleep as studied by human brain potentials. *Journal of Experimental Psychology*, 21, 127–144.

LUCE, G.G. (1971) *Body Time: The Natural Rhythms of the Body*. St. Albans: Paladin.

LUCE, G.G. & SEGAL, J. (1966) *Sleep*. New York: Coward, McCann & Geoghegan.

LUGARESSI, E., MEDORI, R., MONTAGNA, P., BARUZZI, A., CORTELLI, P., LUGARESSI, A., TINUPER, A., ZUCCONI, M. & GAMBETTI, P. (1986) Fatal familial insomnia and dysautonomia in the selective degeneration of thalamic nuclei. *New England Journal of Medicine*, 315, 997–1003.

MARKS, M. & FOLKHARD, S. (1985) Diurnal rhythms in cognitive performance. In J. Nicholson & H. Beloff (Eds) *Psychology Survey 5*. Leicester: British Psychological Society.

McWILLIAMS, S.A. & TUTTLE, R.J. (1973) Long-term psychological effects of LSD. *Psychological Bulletin*, 79, 341–351.

MEDDIS, R. (1975) *The Sleep Instinct*. London: Routledge, Kegan & Paul.

MEDDIS, R., PEARSON, A.J.D. & LANFORD, G. (1973) An extreme case of healthy insomnia. *Electroencephalography and Clinical Neurophysiology*, 35, 213–214.

MIHILL, C. (1997) Drugs turn friends into enemies of the young. *The Guardian*, February 25, 4.

MILLAR, S. (1996) You are feeling sleepy. *The Guardian*, 30 July, 14.

MILLER, N., GOLD, M. & MILLIMAN, R. (1989) Cocaine. *American Family Physician*, 39, 115–121.

MILLER, R.J., HENNESSY, R.T. & LEIBOWITZ, H.W. (1973) The effect of hypnotic ablation of the background on the magnitude of the Ponzo perspective illusion. *International Journal of Clinical and Experimental Hypnosis*, 21, 18–191.

MINORS, D. (1997) Melatonin – hormone of darkness. *Biological Sciences Review*, 10, 39–41.

MORGAN, E. (1995) Measuring time with a biological clock. *Biological Sciences Review*, 7, 2–5.

MORUZZI, G. & MAGOUN, H.W. (1949) Reticular formation and activation of the EEG. *Electroencephalography and Clinical Neurophysiology*, 1, 455–473.

NEILL, J. (1987) 'More than medical significance': LSD and American psychiatry 1953 to 1966. *Journal of Psychoactive Drugs*, 19, 39–45.

OAKLEY, D., ALDEN, P. & MATHER, M.M. (1996) The use of hypnosis in therapy with adults. *The Psychologist*, 9, 502–505.

ORNE, M. (1959) The nature of hypnosis: Artifact and essence. *Journal of Abnormal and Social Psychology*, 58, 277–299.

ORNE, M.T. & EVANS, F.J. (1965) Social control in the psychological experiment: Anti-social behaviour and hypnosis. *Journal of Personality and Social Psychology*, 1, 189–200.

ORNE, M.T., SHEEHAN, P.W. & EVANS, F.J. (1968) Occurrence of posthypnotic behaviour outside the experimental setting. *Journal of Personality and Social Psychology*, 9, 189–196.

OSWALD, I. (1966) *Sleep*. Harmondsworth: Penguin.

PARROTT, A. (1997) Ecstatic but memory depleted? *The Psychologist*, 10, 265.

PARROTT, A. & YEOMANS, M. (1995) Wobble, rave, inhale or crave. *The Psychologist*, 8, 305.

PATRICK, G.T.W. & GILBERT, J.A. (1898) On the effects of loss of sleep. The *Psychological Review*, 3, 469–483.

PATTIE, F.A. (1937) The genuineness of hypnotically produced anaesthesia of the skin. *American Journal of Psychology*, 49, 435–443.

PENGELLEY, E.T. & FISHER, K.C. (1957) Onset and cessation of hibernation under constant temperature and light in the golden-mantled ground squirrel, Citellus Lateralis. *Nature*, 180, 1371–1372.

RECHTSCHAFFEN, A., GILLILAND, M., BERGMANN, B. & WINTER, J. (1983) Physiological correlates of prolonged sleep deprivation in rats. *Science*, 221, 182–184.

RECHTSCHAFFEN, A. & KALES, A. (1968) A manual of standardised terminology, techniques, and scoring system for sleep stages of human subjects. *National Institute of Health Publication 204*. Washington, DC: US Government Printing Office.

REINBERG, A. (1967) Eclairement et cycle menstruel de la femme. Rapport au Colloque International du CRNS, la photoregulation de la reproduction chez les oiseaux et les mammifères, Montpelier.

REISER, M. & NIELSEN, M. (1980) Investigative hypnosis: A developing speciality. *American Journal of Clinical Hypnosis*, 23, 75–83.

ROGERS, B. (1994) Let them eat raw onions. *The Sunday Telegraph*, 13 November, 6.

ROSSI, E.I. (1973) The dream protein hypothesis. *American Journal of Psychiatry*, 130, 1094–1097.

RUBIN, F. (Ed.) (1968) *Current Research in Hypnopaedia*. New York: Elsevier.

RYBACK, R.S. & LEWIS, O.F. (1971) Effects of prolonged bed rest on EEG sleep patterns in young, healthy volunteers. *Electroencephalography and Clinical Neurophysiology*, 31, 395–399.

SABBAGH, K. & BARNARD, C. (1984) *The Living Body*. London: Macdonald.

SHAPIRO, C.M., BORTZ, R., MITCHELL, D., BARTEL, P. & JOOSTE, P. (1981) Slow-wave sleep: A recovery period after exercise. *Science*, 214, 1253–1254.

SIEGEL, R.K. (1982) Quoted by Hooper, J. in 'Mind tripping'. *Omni*, October, 155.

SMITH, D.E., WESSON, D.R., BUXTON, M.E., SEYMOUR, R. & KRAMER, H.M. (1978) The diagnosis and treatment of the PCP abuse syndrome. In R.C. Peterson & R.C. Stillman (Eds) *Phencyclidine (PCP) Abuse: An Appraisal*. NIDA Research Monograph No. 21, DHEW Publication No. ADM 78–728. Washington, DC: US Government Printing Office.

SNYDER, S. (1977) Opiate receptors and internal opiates. *Scientific American*, 236, 44–56.

SPANOS, N.P. (1986) Hypnotic behaviour: A social-psychological interpretation of amnesia, analgesia, and 'trance logic'. *The Behavioural and Brain Sciences*, 9, 499–502.

SPANOS, N.P. (1991) A sociocognitive approach to hypnosis. In S.J. Lynn & J.W. Rhue (Eds) *Theories of Hypnosis: Current Models and Perspectives*. New York: Guildford Press.

SPANOS, N.P., GWYNN, M.I. & STAM, H.J. (1983) Instructional demands and ratings of overt and hidden pain during hypnotic analgesia. *Journal of Abnormal Psychology*, 92, 479–488.

SPANOS, N.P., JONES, B. & MALFARA, A. (1982) Hypnotic deafness: Now you hear it – now you still hear it. *Journal of Abnormal Psychology*, 91, 75–77.

TILLEY, A.J. & EMPSON, J.A.C. (1978) REM sleep and memory consolidation. *Biological Psychology*, 6, 293–300.

TIMONEN, S., FRANZAS, B. & WISCHMANN, K. (1964) Photosensibility of the human pituitary. *Annales Chirurgiae et Gynaecologiae Feminae*, 53, 156–172.

WAGSTAFF, G.F. (1991) Compliance, belief, and semantics in hypnosis: A non-state sociocognitive perspective. In S.J. Lynn & J.W. Rhue (Eds) *Theories of Hypnosis: Current Models and Perspectives*. New York: Guildford Press.

WEBB, W.B. (1975) *Sleep: The Gentle Tyrant*. Englewood Cliffs, NJ: Prentice-Hall.

WEBB, W.B. (1982) Sleep and biological rhythms. In Webb, W.B. (Ed.) *Biological Rhythms, Sleep and Performance*. Chichester: John Wiley & Sons.

WEBB, W.B. & CAMPBELL, S. (1983) Relationships in sleep characteristics of identical and fraternal twins. *Archives of General Psychiatry*, 40, 1093–1095.

WEBB, W.B. & CARTWRIGHT, R.D. (1978) Sleep and dreams. *Annual Review of Psychology*, 29, 223–252.

WEHR, T. & ROSENTHAL, N. (1989) Seasonability and affective illness. *American Journal of Psychiatry*, 146, 201–204.

WEIL, A. & ROSEN, W. (1983) *Chocolate to Morphine: Understanding Mind-Active Drugs*. Boston: Houghton Mifflin.

INDEX